YOUR HEALING HANDS

The Polarity Experience

by Richard Gordon

Illustrations by Meg Studer

Unity Press   Santa Cruz

Published by Unity Press
113 New Street, Santa Cruz, CA 95060

First printing 1978

Cover photography & art: Franklin L. Avery and John Ploeger

This book does not intend to treat, diagnose, or prescribe, and therefore does not take responsibility for your experiences using this system.

Gordon, Richard, 1948–
   Your healing hands. 1. Mental/Physical healing. I. Title.   II. Title: the Polarity experience. [DNLM: 1. Therapeutic WB890 G664y]   RZ401.G74   615'.851
78–12527   ISBN 0–913300–07–1

Printed in the United States of America
      5   6   7   8   9

Dedication

This book is dedicated to all my teachers and friends who have helped to make this book a reality. Most of all, I dedicate it to you, the reader, and the discovery of your own healing hands.

Table of Contents

Preface

This book is an introduction to polarity energy balancing. I stress the word introduction. The polarity system is vast—like an unexplored continent or even a new branch of science. There is considerably more theory and information on this subject than could be presented in these few pages. The purpose of this text is to introduce you to the polarity system and explore your healing potential, and to expand the boundaries within which we experience ourselves.

Our Hands Are A Gift

Through them, we can channel the
love in our hearts to relieve the
suffering of those around us.

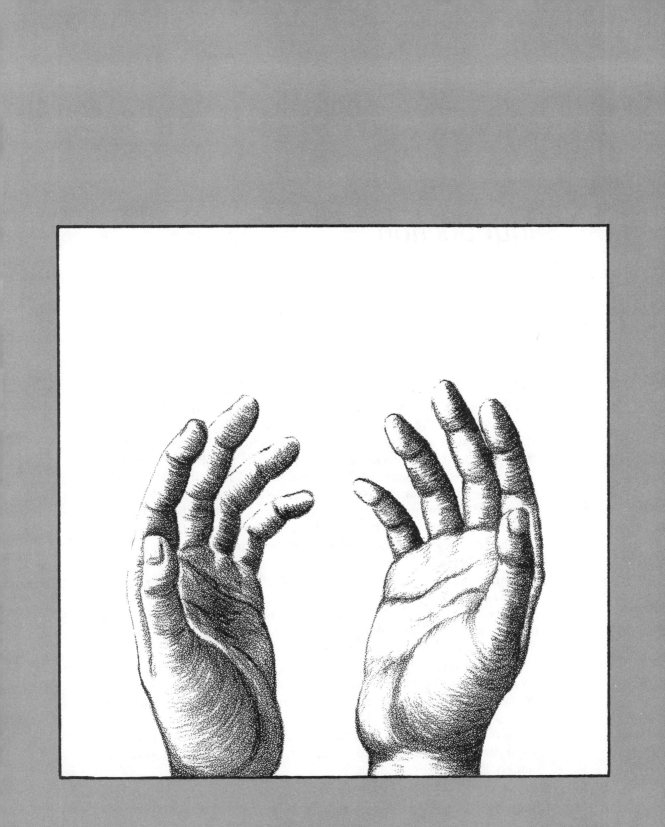

Introduction

Once there was a boy who discovered that within his hand he held a small seed. He planted the seed, and it started to grow. After a few weeks, he said, "Behold, this seed grows into a green vine!" A few days later, the green vine started sending graceful shoots into the air. Then the boy said, "Aha, so this is a green vine with beautiful shoots." He believed this until summer when the plant brought forth hundreds of gold, yellow, blue, orange and red flowers. "Now I know what this is," said the boy. "It's a green vine with beautiful shoots producing many flowers of bright colors." By fall, the vine was covered with lovely purple fruit that was exquisite to the taste.

Polarity has been like that vine for me. Every time I rediscover it, it becomes more wonderful. Describing it to people who have never experienced it is like describing rare gems to those who have never seen or held them. It is like describing color to a blind man; he may get an idea of what you say, but until he sees, he will not understand.

To know there is something I can give, something that flows through my hands to help others experience life and health more fully, has been a source of great joy in my life. I never feel helpless when I see a friend in pain.

It is remarkable, as I jog back in memory, to realize how surprised I was when that small seed I planted began to grow, branch out and flower so quickly.

While still in college, I felt that my studies were too abstract to be directly nourishing to my life. I wanted to be able to personalize what I was learning and to express my creative potential, and not merely regurgitate facts for the purpose of passing examinations. My intentions were to create a simple and gratifying lifestyle, to express myself with love and honesty and to move past my fears and explore the mysteries inside and outside myself. To do this, I left college to pursue a course of independent study. Over the last ten years, I have been deeply involved in the personal growth movement. Yet, my initial interest in natural healing and polarity energy balancing began only when I became mindful of my own health.

I moved from California to live in the mountains of Mexico above the town of Tepoztlán. The people living there had a certain delightful spirit, free from the neurotic pace and paranoia I had grown up with for over two decades in Los Angeles. During this time, I studied yoga, nutrition, herbs, fasting, and spiritual writings. To supplement my education, I traveled to the Christos School of Natural Healing in Taos, New Mexico and studied under Dr. William LeSassier, ND. We studied herbal medicine and therapeutic techniques such as acupressure, reflexology, shiatzu, deep muscle massage, lymphatic massage, and selected chiropractic adjustments, as well as methods of relaxation, visualization, and meditation for healing. I had no special expectations when we were introduced to polarity, as all these different techniques seemed very worthwhile.

We had been studying polarity for two days when I woke up on the morning of the third day feeling quite poorly. I felt so bad, in fact, that I didn't want to talk to anyone. It was on that particular morning that my friend Valerie offered to give me a full polarity session.

Valerie worked on me for forty minutes, and the polarity lifted me from feeling barely alive to completely wonderful. I was deeply impressed!

I learned that the polarity system has a holistic approach to health and healing. This means it deals with the whole person: thoughts and attitudes, nutritional needs, special exercises known as "polarity yoga," and, of course, the polarity session to facilitate the body in healing itself. When I started giving polarity sessions, I must admit I found it hard to believe that holding my hands over someone could possibly be of any benefit to them. My understanding had been that only an especially gifted person could heal others with their hands. In spite of my skepticism, which lasted for more than a year, I consistently got good results.

One week after completing the general polarity training session, I encountered a woman in great pain from what her doctor had diagnosed as a tubular pregnancy. I told her I had just learned something called polarity that might help her relax. "Anything!" she responded. "I'll try anything!"

Half an hour later, she was saying, "I can't believe these are my hands! I can't believe these are my feet! I feel great!" A few days later she brought me a loaf of bread she had baked—and the news that her doctor had said that, although he didn't understand it, somehow her condition seemed to be fine.

That same week, Dr. LeSassier was demonstrating neck adjustments. The adjustment could not be made on one woman because she held too much tension in her neck. He told us that a full adjustment would require a couple of weeks of deep massage. Her neck was hurting after the demonstration, so I gave her some polarity. Fifteen minutes later, I called Dr. LeSassier over. He confirmed that the bones in her neck had shifted back into place and asked what I had done. "I gave her some polarity," I said. Since then I have witnessed many instances where misaligned bones have literally fallen back into place following a polarity session.

Once a woman came to a class I was starting. She said that despite competent medical attention over the previous fifteen years, her physical condition had grown progressively worse. She was desperate for help. After giving the group a brief introductory talk on polarity, I selected five of the new students, and we formed a polarity circle around the woman. When we were done, she looked ten years younger. Her face was relaxed. Her hands had stopped shaking. She told us she had not felt such peace, such calmness, for thirty years. For the first time in memory, she could lie on her back without her knees up in the air. And she had perspired, she explained, without medication—for the first time since childhood. A week later, she returned to report that an x-ray taken after her polarity session showed that half of the double backward s-curve in her spine had straightened out.

Time and again I was surprised and impressed by the effectiveness of the polarity method. One woman, three weeks late with her period, was told by her doctor that she had a uterine infection. I started giving her a polarity, and while I was working on her feet, four children asked if they could help. I placed them in the various positions of the polarity circle. Twenty minutes later her period started, and she got up feeling very relieved. She reported that each time one of the children touched her, she had experienced a surge of golden light flowing through her body.

During a lecture, I was demonstrating the tummy rock move on a middle-aged woman. When I stopped the rocking, I felt tremendous energy moving through my hands, so I asked her if she felt tingling in her body. "No," she replied. Polarity can be very unpredictable but it always does *something*, so I asked if there was any part of her body where she felt energy. "Yes," she said, "I'm feeling a tingling in my hands." "Is there any reason your hands need energy?" I asked. She shook her head. Ten minutes later she excitedly interrupted my talk to exclaim, "The arthritis pain in my hands is gone!" She had become so accustomed to pain in her hands that she hadn't even thought to mention it when I questioned her.

With astonishment, I learned that polarity will ease emotional upsets as well. One extreme example was a man who had taken LSD and began experiencing himself as a total failure in his life. He was deeply upset and near hysteria. After a short polarity, he sat up and said he was feeling much better. "I was blowing things far out of proportion," he realized. Polarity seemed to have relaxed and centered him, drawing his mind back from morbid fantasies under the influence of a powerful hallucinogen.

On another occasion I witnessed how a simple polarity move, the tummy rock, worked wonders for a hyperactive child when used on a daily basis. Each morning about the same time, this little boy would go out of control—to the point where a therapist described his behavior as hysterical. I taught the therapist the tummy rock. First she had to catch the boy and force him to lie down so she could do the move. After a few minutes of polarity, the boy would fall sound asleep for an hour or two. Upon awakening, he was relaxed and able to interact normally with other children. Sometimes he would even apologize to the others for his rude behavior. The therapist was so impressed that she taught the boy's mother to use the tummy rock—with gratifying results.

Polarity effects are not always instantaneous, or so dramatic. People with chronic conditions often need a series of sessions in conjunction with an improved diet, exercise, and most important, positive attitudes and emotions. Sometimes a person may temporarily feel worse before feeling better. Other times a person may not appear to be helped at all. My next door neighbor was a good example of this. One day he had strained his back while exercising, and his pain was so great that he couldn't even roll over. I gave him a complete polarity session, but when it was over, he felt no relief. Somewhat concerned, I contacted one of my teachers and related what happened. "Oh, didn't I tell you?" she laughed. "It takes about twenty-four hours for polarity to work on the back." The next morning, my neighbor was out in front of his house, chopping wood.

What I have shared here is but a small sampling of the many experiences I have had. Each time I saw the effects of polarity surpass my highest expectations, my faith in polarity increased. Now I recognize that we all have the power to assist in healing—not through magic—but through a simple science of energy, an energy magnified by our love.

Receiving

Exposed, developed and fixed film is no longer
sensitive to light. So put aside exposed, developed, and fixed concepts, and receive this
gift. For the moment, empty your cup so that
it may be filled.

SECTION I

Polarity

Polarity energy balancing is a simple and effective method used to bring on deep healing relaxation. It is easy to learn, subtle, powerful, safe and fun.

By employing the currents of life-force that naturally flow through everyone's hands, we can release and balance another person's energy. As long as this energy is flowing freely, we experience peace, joy, love and health.

Life-Force

Life-force is a subtle form of electromagnetic energy. It is the animating current of life and a physiological reality in the body.

Through the centuries, life-force has been called different names by many people. It is not a recent discovery. Christ called it 'light'; the Russians in their psychic research have called it 'bioplasmic' energy; Wilhelm Reich referred to it as 'orgone energy'; East Indian yogis call it 'pran' or 'prana'; Reichenbach spoke of it as 'odic force'; to the Kahunas, it is 'mana'; Paracelsus called it 'munia'; the usual Chinese term is 'chi' or 'ki'; alchemists' manuscripts speak of 'vital fluid'; Eeman described it as 'x-force'; Bruner named it 'bio-cosmic' energy; Hippocrates called it

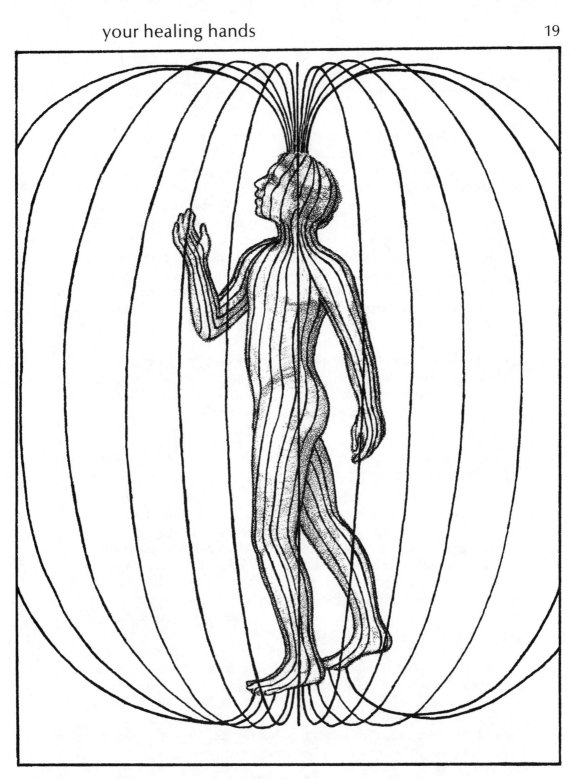

Life-force can be thought of as a circulating energy field surrounding and penetrating the body. It is the animating current of life and is naturally directed by the body's intelligence.

'*vis medicatrix naturae*' (nature's life force). It also has other names like bio-energy, cosmic energy, vital force, ether of space, etc. I'm sure there are numerous others. For the sake of simplicity, we will refer to it as life-force, or just 'the energy'.

Life-force flows through the body as if it were following an invisible circulatory system, charging every cell in its path. This current of energy can become weakened and partially blocked due to stress. The science of acupuncture involves locating the exact points where blockage occurs and, using needles, stimulates these points to restore flow. In polarity energy balancing, physical and nonphysical touch techniques are used to send energy through the entire system to open up the blocked points. This reestablishes the proper flow and alignment of life-force throughout the body.

Energy is energy. There is no bad energy—only well-directed or mis-directed energy. Polarity directs the life-force along its natural pathways to untangle 'energy knots' caused by physical or emotional stress. Polarity brings on deep healing relaxation at all levels.

Experiencing the Force

Many people wonder why they had never been aware of life-force in the past. Imagine a group of people who, when looking at the colors orange and red, had always called them both red. If someone came along one day and pointed out the difference between the two colors, suddenly everyone would see the distinction. Well, the life-force has always been a part of our lives, but as in the hypothetical example of the colors, we have not bothered to differentiate it from the overall physical sensations that we are accustomed to experiencing.

Life-force can be easily experienced. Rub your hands vigorously together for a minute. Now hold them a few inches apart. Move your hands together and apart, between one to six inches, and see where you feel the strongest energy. It may be felt as a tingling, vibrating, hot or cold type of sensation, or as a magnetic field.

Have a friend rub his hands together too, and then have him place one hand between your two. Move your hands in and out, one to six inches

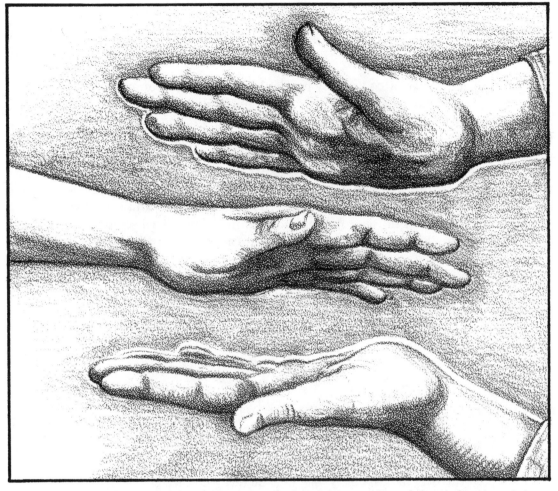

Sometimes the experience of the life-force is only slightly perceptible, while at other times it is intense. If you do not feel it the first time, try again with someone else.

from his. Within a few seconds to a minute, you will most likely be feeling something. If, for example, you experience tingling in a spot by your thumbs when your friend's palm is directly between yours, your friend will most likely experience tingling in exactly that part of the hand immediately between the places where you feel it.

When you start using polarity on friends or family members, the experience of the tingling and vibrating in your hands will at times become far more powerful than the effects you may have just experienced. I have often held my hands above another person in one of the polarity moves when suddenly my hands felt incredible rushes of surging and tingling energy. My sensations correspond to the sensations of the other person, who simultaneously feels the energy surging and tingling through his or her body.

The more relaxed you are, the easier it is to feel the life-force as it passes through your hands. The more relaxed your friend is when you are channeling, the more effective the polarity will be, and your own experience of the life-force will be magnified. Don't be discouraged if you don't feel the life-force at first, as it isn't always strongly felt. As you continue to work with the life-force you will become increasingly aware of it.

How to Stop a Headache

Stopping a tension headache is so easy, anyone can do it! If you are with someone who has a headache, here's what you can do.

Rub your hands briskly together and feel your own energy. Next, gently touch the palm of your right hand to the back of the person's neck. Hold your left hand one-half inch away from his or her forehead. Ask your friend to take ten deep breaths and let each one out with a sigh. Your friend's deep breathing will increase the feeling of life-force that you will feel in your hands. If it doesn't, have them repeat the breathing again. Leave your hands in place as long as you can feel a strong energy transference. Within three to five minutes, most headaches will be gone or greatly relieved. If the headache persists, it will be necessary to do a more complete polarity—as shown in the polarity one-to-one section on page 38.

When you are finished, shake your hands forcefully—as if you were throwing off water—then wash your hands in cold water to remove static energy.

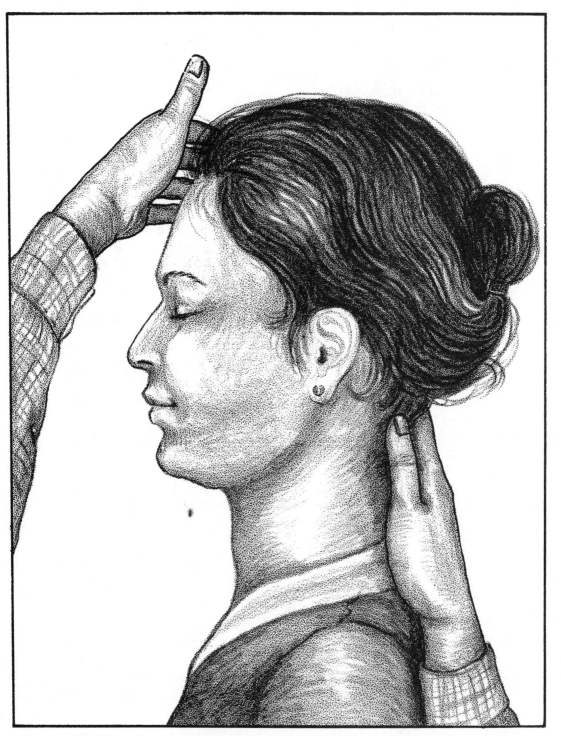

Stopping a headache: You may experience the tingle of life-force more dramatically in your left hand in this position because it is not physically touching the forehead of your friend.

History of Polarity

Dr. Randolph Stone, the originator of the modern polarity system, was born in Austria in 1890. He immigrated to America with his father, settled in Chicago and became a citizen.

Dr. Stone became a doctor of osteopathy, a doctor of naturopathy and a chiropractor as well, maintaining a private practice from 1914 to 1972. Despite all this training, Dr. Stone was unsatisfied with the Western approach to healing and felt a need to explore other healing techniques. In China and France he studied acupuncture and herbology. In the Orient, he learned reflexology and other Eastern massage techniques. In the course of his work, he stumbled across the ancient Spagyric art of healing as taught by the great Doctor Paracelsus von Hohenheim, who had studied in Arabia. This provided Dr. Stone with essential knowledge of subtle electromagnetic fields of the body. Over the course of sixty years, Dr. Stone integrated this wealth of knowledge into a system he named Polarity Therapy.

At the age of eighty-four, Dr. Randolph Stone retired to live in India, appointing Pierre Pannetier, a naturopathic doctor, as his successor to direct the future growth of polarity therapy.

The intent of this book is not to represent the teachings of Dr. Randolph Stone. The information presented in this work demonstrates successful innovations and variations of polarity energy balancing that have evolved from Dr. Stone's pioneering achievements.

The Principle of Polarity

Just as the earth and sun have north and south magnetic poles, so do our bodies. In fact, everything that stands upright on the planet has a positive charge on top, and a negative charge at the base.

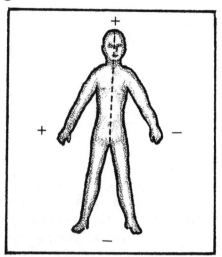

Polarity patterns in the body follow electromagnetic principles found throughout nature.

The top of the body has a positive charge.
The feet have a negative charge.
The right side has a positive charge.
The left side has a negative charge.
(These charges are commonly measured using sensitive voltmeters.)

When the positive and negative poles of magnets are put together, there is an attractive current between them. Similarly, polarity energy is directed magnetically along its lines of force to align and establish the vital polarities of the body. Blocked areas create an imbalance in the body's natural energy field, an imbalance which the polarity practitioner treats by connecting:

the right (+) hand to the left (−) side of the body, and by connecting:

the left (−) hand to the right (+) side of the body.

Again, if you are working with someone, *your right hand goes to their left side, and your left hand goes to their right side.*

If you are working on the vertical center line of the body, the left (−) hand is always placed above in a relatively more positive area, and the right (+) hand is placed below in a relatively more negative area.

Again, when working the vertical center line of the body, your left hand goes above, and your right hand goes below.

Results

When giving a polarity, you will see the greatest results when a person needs help the most. A healthy, happy person who experiences polarity will probably feel very relaxed and at peace, while someone who is very much out of balance will often feel completely rejuvenated.

Polarity energy balancing recharges the life-force in a person. This balances the subtle electromagnetic aura fields around the body. When the aura is balanced, the nerves are relaxed. The nerves control the muscles, and the muscles hold the bones. It is not at all surprising to see bones literally fall back into place after a polarity.

Here is a way for you to see this for yourself. When your friend is lying on his or her back, note the position of each foot before the polarity begins. Are they even, or do they go off at different angles? In many cases a polarity session will properly align the bones, so the two feet will be noticeably more even.

Because polarity works on such deep levels, do not be surprised to see very great changes in the person you are working on. Emotionally upset people may start releasing, forgiving and relaxing. If a person wants to cry, it should be gently encouraged. Other people may go into a very deep state of conscious sleep. Allow a person to rest as long as she or he likes. If it is cold, be sure to cover the person. Sometimes, people feel like getting a night's rest after the polarity. Other times, people feel as if they have just awakened from a night's rest. Sometimes a person may feel very hot or may shiver as blood is directed toward the skin or to internal organs. Sometimes, people go into states of bliss or ecstasy. Whatever happens, be confident that it is exactly what that person needs at that time. Life-force will go only where it is needed to bring on the changes that are necessary. It makes people feel better.

Life-force does not differentiate between physical and emotional pain. Both are simply expressions of blocked life-force. Over the years, I have watched polarity help the young and old suffering from many different conditions. In many cases, polarity offers effective pain relief without medication.

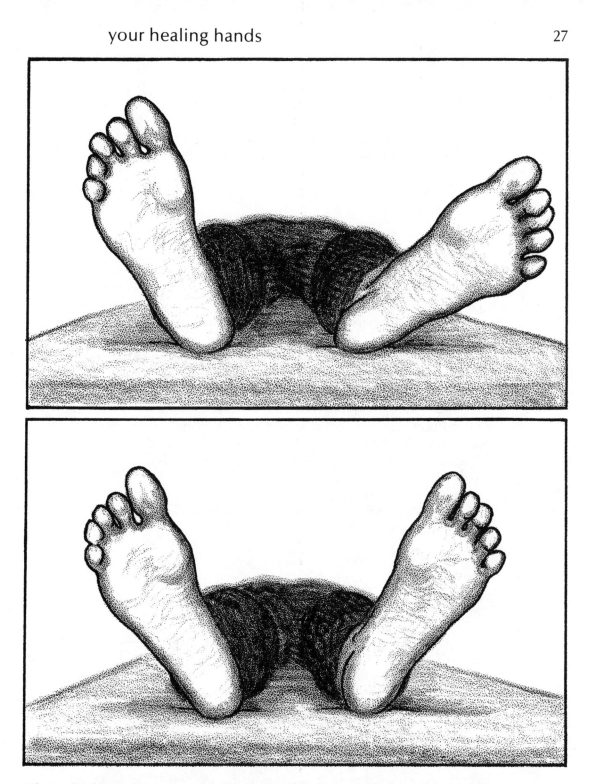

The angle of one's feet suggest the positioning of the bones in the hips. Polarity sessions can induce such profound relaxation that the bones will often change their position and alter the angle of the feet. The result is a visible improvement in posture.

People giving polarity sessions are circulating life-force, so they too may experience benefits. When a circuit of love is created, all in the circle are uplifted.

Chronic Conditions

In chronic conditions and in severe situations, a series of polarities is highly recommended. Do not expect instant results from the polarity. It took perhaps ten, twenty, or fifty years to get the system so far out of balance. Therefore, it may take a series of polarities plus improved attitudes, exercise and nutritional habits to bring about the necessary changes. You may, however, get instant results in the form of pain relief or better functioning of the system.

A polarity session three or four times a week can work wonders. When the condition has shown definite signs of improvement, two polarities a week will suffice. For those who appear to be healed, one polarity a week as a tonic is an excellent idea until all symptoms are completely eliminated.

It's good to ask the person receiving the polarities how often they feel polarities are of benefit. Remember, it is far better to give a series of polarities than an occasional one.

Elders

When giving polarity to the elderly, there are special considerations. Frequent short polarities are most appropriate and beneficial. A strong polarity by itself could start a healing cleansing process, releasing long-accumulated toxins which the older person may not have enough life-force to eliminate. It's much better to go slowly and easily.

Along with frequent sessions—i.e. three times a week—a cleansing diet is essential for seniors. Well-researched and clear information on this subject is provided in books I recommend to the reader on page 129.

Children

Children love to give and receive polarities. We call polarity 'giving love' as an explanation to children, and the polarity circle is called a 'love circle'. Youngsters can instantly feel the life-force. They are generally more sensitive and have much less conditioning to block the experience. Polarity is extremely effective on children because they are open to letting love flow through them. Furthermore, it doesn't take much to balance the energy in their small bodies.

The polarity circle is in many ways ideal for children. It is easy to teach, and provides children with an opportunity to love and serve others in a non-threatening way. The circle is painless and fun. Make sure children rinse their hands in cold water after giving a polarity. The finishing moves in the one-to-one session also work very well for children. Some little ones will tolerate mild pressure moves. Whatever you do, let the polarity experience be enjoyable for them.

Since bedtime is a frequent problem for many small children—and their parents—the following example may be put to good use. One day a friend of mine introduced her three-year-old daughter to polarity when the child was in a calm pleasant mood. Using the tummy rock, Sarah's mother called it "giving love', and Sarah enjoyed it immensely. A few nights later when her daughter was in a cranky mood, my friend asked her, "Would you like mommy to give you some love?" By the time the tummy rock was over, Sarah was sound asleep.

From that time, bedtime has never been a problem. Every night Sarah insists that her mother 'give her some love' before she goes to sleep. This simple and effective polarity move not only helps Sarah get to sleep without making a fuss, but is also highly beneficial to her health on a preventative level as it aligns her life-force field each night.

Getting Wet

You don't need to believe that this system
will work, in order to profoundly experience
it. You don't need to believe in the ocean
to get wet; however, you do have to jump in.

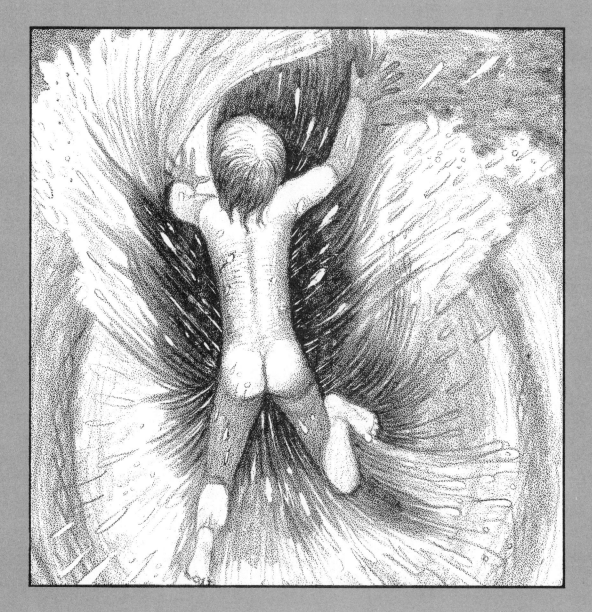

SECTION II

Polarity One-to-One

This section of the book will describe how one person can give a powerful polarity session to another person. Later, we will explore how a group of six people using non-pressure and non-touch polarity techniques, can bring on major physical changes in the body. *I recommend that you carefully read through the first section of this book before going on.*

Types of Touch

Polarity one-to-one uses three types of touch: deep massage, light non-pressure touch and non-physical touch, where the hands are placed slightly away from the body.

Life-force flows in a subtle circulatory system throughout the body. When there is stress because of worry or fear over work or personal problems, the flow of life-force tends to become congested in various places, leaving the rest of the body without sufficient energy to function well. Deep pressure can release the blocked life-force. After the energy is released and flowing freely, light touch and non-touch techniques can polarize the energy—that is, organize and align the life-force along its proper pathways.

Attitudes

When giving a polarity, the best attitude is a relaxed and loving one.
Although the life-force is affected by our thoughts, it is not essential to
concentrate, meditate, or try in any way to do a good job. The energy
flows all by itself, of its own doing. It is helpful to center yourself. This
means to gather your attention and be aware of what you are doing. If
you try hard to do a good job, you will not be relaxed and you will only
block the flow of life-force. The best approach is to simply 'be' with the
person receiving it. You can like the person, love the person, or just feel
good inside. With any of these attitudes, the life-force will flow freely.

*Don't give a polarity session if you feel negatively toward the person
who will receive it, if you are going through severe emotional turmoil,
or if you are ill.* These are wonderful times to *receive* a polarity, however!

Polarity energy balancing is not faith-healing and it works quite well
for skeptics. Disbelieving in polarity will not alter your life-force signifi-
cantly, provided that you feel good inside while you do it. Polarity oper-
ates according to universal principles of life-force and electromagnetic
attraction, not by our opinions.

Self-Protection

When working with the subtle energy of life-force, it is necessary to take
a few minor precautions to be sure you don't pick up static energy from
another person.

First, *know that you are not the healer.* This becomes very evident to
me when I am using a non-physical technique such as the cradle or the
tummy rock. At times, my hands suddenly heat up, and I feel a force
field a few inches thick around them, with a river of energy vibrating
between me and my friend. I don't know where it is going or what it is
doing. It is the life-force that is doing the healing, not me as a person. All
I do is put my hands in position and watch what happens. The love

within us in the form of life-force does the healing. So a good attitude to have is 'let it happen', or if you prefer, 'Thy will be done'. Just take the position as an observer. Even a skeptical observer will do fine. Thinking 'I am a healer', puts out an attractive vibration of 'I', 'I', 'I', which can attract static energy from the person receiving the polarity to the person giving the polarity.

Second, *shake your hands and rinse them in cold water*. When you finish giving a polarity, it is necessary to shake your hands a few times with a strong downward thrust, as if you were throwing off water. Next, rinse your hands in cold water. These two steps remove and ground the static, non-directed energy that may be on your hands. Static energy may be felt as heaviness, thickness, or as a swollen feeling in your hands.

Third, *do not give a polarity session if you are very tired or spaced-out*. Being spaced-out is a condition in which you do not feel 'present' in your bodily experience, a feeling of being not quite there. Under these conditions you will be more susceptible to picking up your friend's energy, a transference which is undesirable and to be avoided.

Fourth, *have a sense of trust in the process*. Don't worry if something unusual happens. A person may feel worse before feeling better, he or she may suddenly go into a deep sleep, perhaps become very cold, or have sensations throughout the body that have never been felt before. Know that the life-force is connected with the body's intelligence to do what is needed. On rare occasions while giving a polarity session, you may even feel symptoms of the other person in your own body. Do not be afraid! Just observe it happening, and the experience will pass through you within a minute.

Magnetic Effect

You usually feel great after giving a polarity session. There are occasions however, when you may feel tired afterwards. This indicates that you were not relaxed during the session. The life-force that you passed on to the other person will be helpful. So relax, take a little break and a few deep breaths. Some vigorous exercise and a cool shower can be helpful, and your strength will soon return.

Atmosphere

When giving a polarity, see that the room is warm, quiet and comfortable, with sufficient space in which to move around. It's best to limit distractions if possible. Unplug the telephone, remove pets, and put up a 'do not disturb' sign, etc. For a treat, put on some soothing music.

Clothing

Wear loose, comfortable clothing.

The person receiving the polarity should take off his or her shoes and socks. This allows direct energy contact with the feet. For comfort's sake, it's helpful for those giving a polarity to take off their shoes as well.

It is advisable to remove all metal from clothes and body when you give or receive a polarity. The metal seems to interfere slightly with the flow of life-force. Put aside jewelry, belt buckles, keys, change, watches and any other metallic objects before starting.

Worktables

Giving a polarity on a massage table is by far the most comfortable way to do it. You can perform all the moves and positions while relaxed and at ease. A makeshift table can be as simple as a door with foam padding over it, placed on two saw horses. Commercial massage tables are excellent and may be purchased through hospital supply stores and other outlets. When selecting a table, make sure it fits your needs. Some features to look for include adjustable height (so it is comfortable for you and so others may use it), sufficient width (so that a large man could lie on his back without his arms falling off), sufficient rigidity, and a weight which would render it portable. One good source for massage tables is Living Earth Crafts, Box 648, Cotati, California 94928.

Starting a Polarity

Before starting a session, let your friend know that all he or she needs to do is to take some deep breaths, relax, and enjoy the experience. Your friend can discuss what he or she is experiencing, laugh, cry, or be silent. The more you can help your friend relax, the more easily life-force will flow through the body. Do whatever feels appropriate at the moment.

Breathing

You can greatly increase the power of polarity by encouraging the person on the receiving end to do some deep breathing during a session. Life-force is in the air, and it can help to recharge the body. Deep breathing

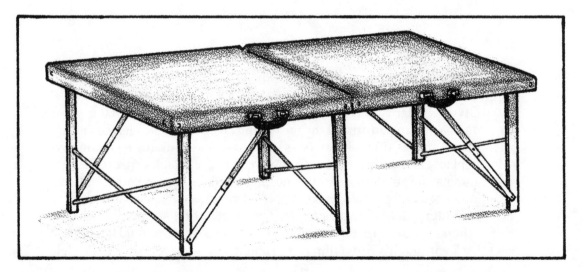

A good massage table is an excellent investment if you plan to do a lot of polarity sessions.

also enables a person to relax and release emotional tightness. *You will discover that when your friend is breathing deeply, you can more dramatically experience the tingle of life-force in the nonphysical moves.* The power of polarity can also be increased by your own breathing patterns. Try deep breathing yourself as you give a polarity. It does not have to be synchronized with the other person's breathing.

While you work, keep a lookout to see that your friend is still breathing deeply. The breath should start from below the navel and go upward all the way to the shoulders. The inhalation should require pulling the air in, while the exhalation should be a totally relaxed, effortless release of breath. During the polarity it's all right if your friend is breathing deeply through either the nose or the mouth.

Learning the Positions

There are a series of positions in the general one-on-one polarity session. They will be most effective if you use them in the order given.

These positions are described in three lessons designed to assist you by dividing the information into easily learned segments. I recommend getting a feel for each lesson and practicing it before going on to the next. In this way, you will quickly be able to learn the general session.

Before you start, read through the title of the move, its description, and the commentary. As you practice, you can skip the commentary section. Later, you will know what the move is just by reading the title. With continued practice, you will remember the entire general polarity session without having to look at the book. Take your time and be patient. The time you spend will be well worth your effort. The one-on-one polarity session offers a perfect opportunity to love someone in a helpful and non-threatening way.

Enjoy

LESSON ONE

POSITION 1 ~ THE CRADLE
Rub your hands briskly together and cradle the head using no pressure.
It's best to *not quite touch the person. Keep your hands relaxed.* The
index and middle fingers go down the sides of the neck, while the
thumbs rest by the ears.

Commentary: The cradle is a very comforting position. It can be of
enormous aid in relieving nervousness, headaches and tension.

*Be sure your body posture is comfortable in this and all other posi-
tions of the polarity session.* Don't strain if your back begins to hurt.
Take a break, come back relaxed and continue.

*Hold this position for as long as you feel a strong energy exchange in
your hands.* There is no set length of time to stay with any of these
positions. You are best to trust your intuitions and feelings. In some
cases, the cradle can be held for half an hour or more. Most often it is
held for a few minutes.

Encourage your friend to breathe deeply. It is easier to experience the
life-force when you are not quite touching your friend.

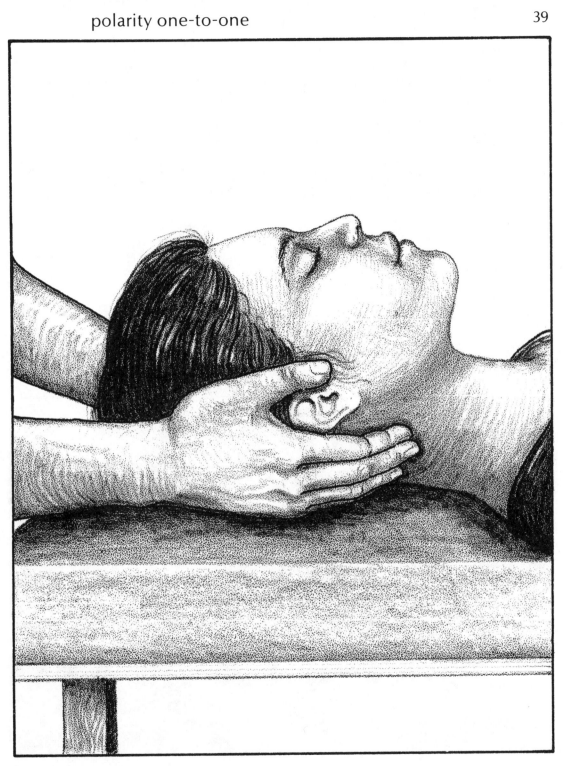

The Cradle

POSITION 2~NORTH POLE STRETCH

Rest your friend's head on the palm of your right hand, so that your middle finger and thumb can take a firm hold on the occipital bone. Your left hand rests on the forehead. With steady pressure, pull straight back with the right hand only. Hold a minute or two.

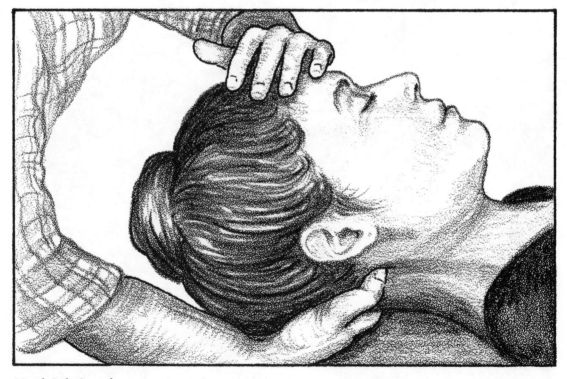

North Pole Stretch

Commentary: Encourage your friend to relax and let you do all the work.

If you feel up along the sides of the back of your neck, you will come across the base of the occipital bone. If you push up under the bone, it will probably be a bit tender. Once having found this place on yourself, it will be easy to find it on another person. When you feel that the thumb and middle finger of your right hand have a solid handle grip on the base of the occipital bone, you know you have it right.

Use as much pressure as your friend can enjoy.

If your right hand gets tired, go on to the next move.

Encourage your friend to breathe deeply if he or she is not doing so.

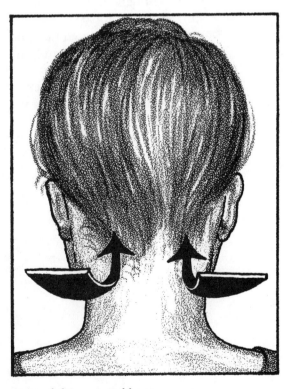

Base of the occipital bone

POSITION 3~TUMMY ROCK

Rub your hands briskly together and from your friend's right side rest your left hand on the forehead, and your right hand just below the navel. Now rock the person rhythmically with the right hand. Rock for a couple of minutes, then stop, and leave your hands in place. Keep your hands there as long as you feel that tingling exchange of life-force (at least a minute). Now lift your hands an inch or two off of your friend and again feel the tingle of life-force in your hands.

Commentary: Make sure that the rocking is even and gentle, like rocking a baby. The whole torso moves an inch or two during the rocking. Follow the momentum of the body to keep a smooth gentle pace. See that your right hand doesn't slide over the surface while the body remains still. Hand and torso should move together. If your friend doesn't seem to rock, try pressing down more deeply with the right hand. When you stop the rocking and leave your hands in place, your friend may feel energy tingling and rushing all through his or her body.

This move is simple and extremely powerful. It is recommended as a treatment if you have only a few minutes. It is wonderful for children before bedtime.

Again, deep and even breathing is very important.

Suggestion: Stop here and try out what you have just read.

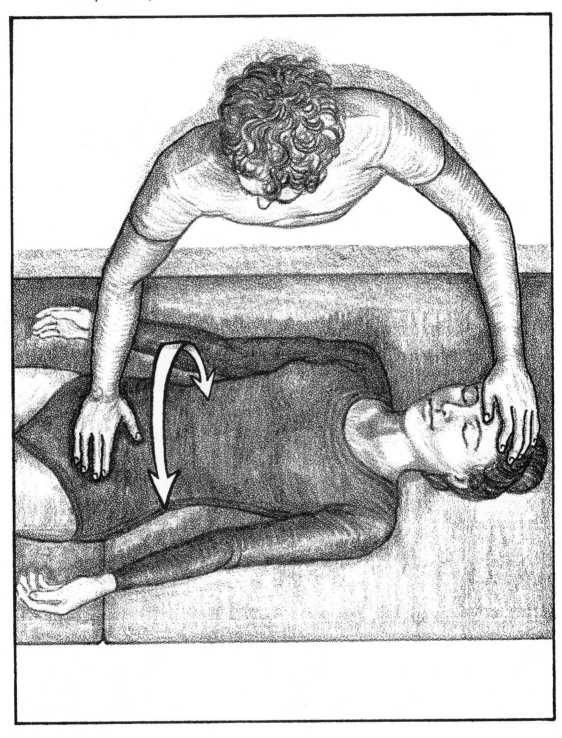

The Tummy Rock

The Feet

Complete all the moves for one foot before starting on the other. The instructions are written for you to begin on your friend's right foot. When you finish the right foot, begin on the left foot, merely reversing the instructions.

POSITION 4~BRUSHING OFF
With both hands, brush down the leg, starting above the knee, and move down to the tips of the toes. Then *shake your hands vigorously* as if you were throwing off water. Repeat this move a few times.

Commentary: This move pulls off static, non-directed energy. Your hands may feel heavy, thick and swollen. This is the time to throw off that energy in a strong flinging manner.

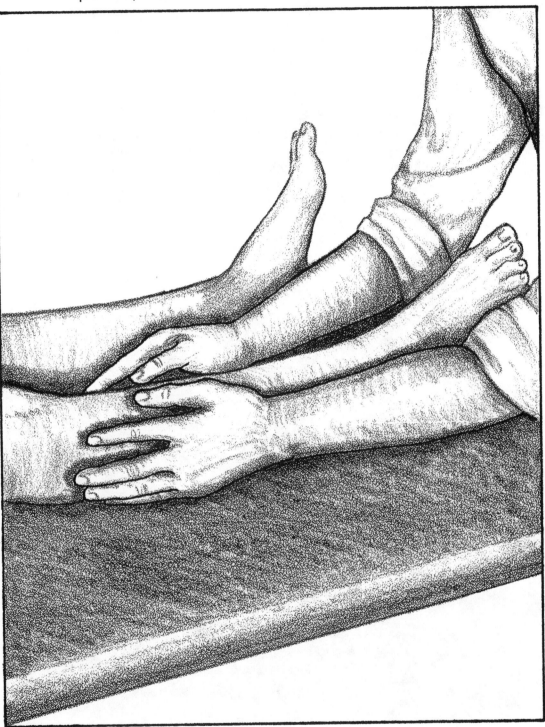

Brushing Off

POSITION 5~LEAN AND PULL

Your friend's right heel sits on the fingers of your left hand. The heel of your right hand is placed on the ball of the foot. Now lean forward on the foot with the power of your right hand, using your body weight to give the Achilles tendon a good stretch. Now place your right hand over the center of the top of the foot and pull downward until the knee raises about one-half inch off the ground. *Be gentle pulling down*. Repeat this a few times.

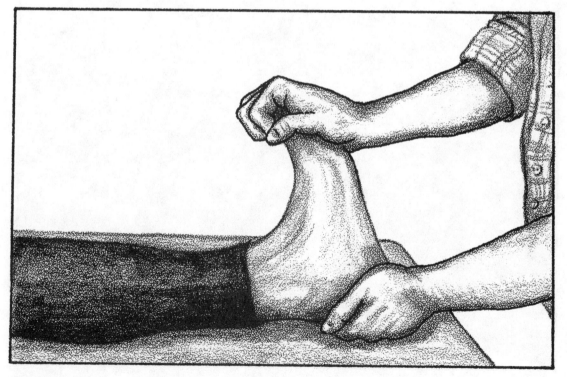

Lean in

Commentary: You can use a great deal of force in the forward motion of this move. However, on the downward pull, be very gentle. Check with your friend to see how it feels.

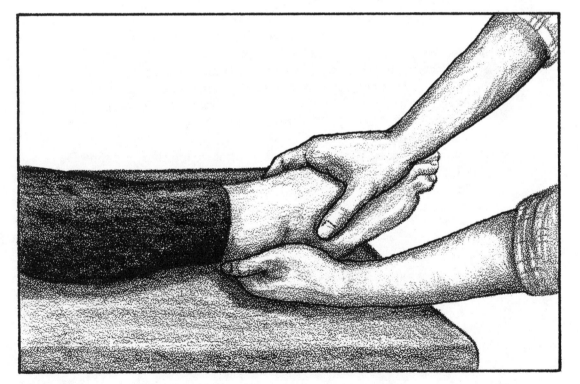

Pull down

POSITION 6~INSIDE HEEL PRESS

Support the heel of the right foot with the fingers of the right hand. With the right thumb, find a sore spot on the inside of the heel. *Press steadily, gently and firmly.* Do *not* massage this spot. Your left hand lightly supports the foot in an upright position.

Commentary: Places that are sore and tender (not from injury) on the feet and other parts of the body, reflect blockages in the flow of life-force through the various organs and systems. Applying pressure to these sore spots will stimulate the flow of life-force through their reflexive organs. (More detailed information on working with sore spots and reflex areas is provided in the section on specific moves.)

Be sure that your thumb nails are short.

It may take a little systematic looking to find a very sore spot. (Caution: see page 89.) Most people have one or more, so investigate the area, and work each one. You may have to apply deep pressure to find sore spots. When your friend acknowledges a painful place, give only the pressure he or she can comfortably tolerate. Encourage your friend to relax and breathe deeply, letting the feelings in the foot go through the rest of the body. As the pain decreases, you can comfortably increase the pressure within a few minutes.

If you feel a pulse under your thumb, move to another sore spot. Do not put direct pressure on a blood vessel.

This move is balancing to the lower pelvic areas in the center of the body, and is especially good for women with menstrual cramps.

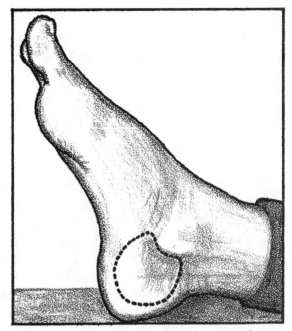

Various sore spots will likely be found in this section of the heel.

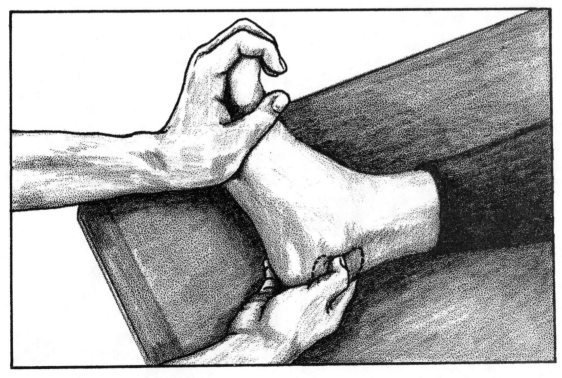

Inside heel press

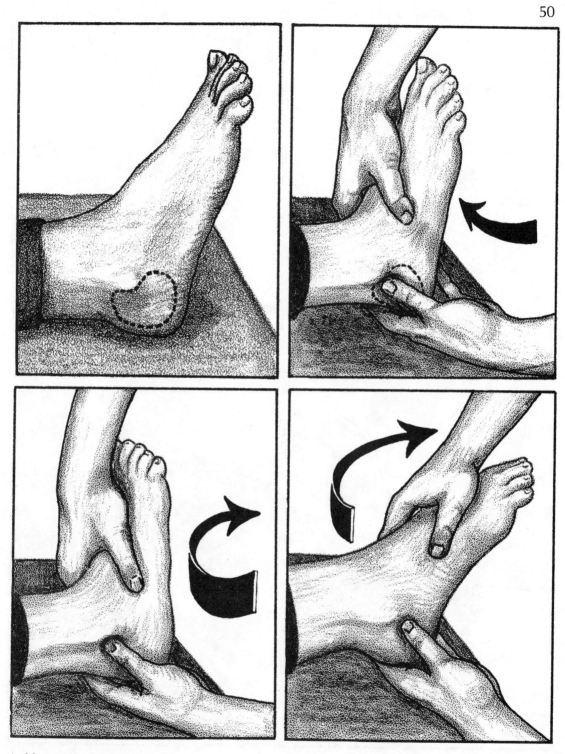

Ankle joint rotates along its axis.

POSITION 7 ~ OUTSIDE HEEL ROTATION
Move to a 45–degree angle from the right foot. Support the heel of the
right foot with the fingers of your left hand. With your left thumb, find
a sore spot on the outside of the heel area. Be sensitive, *apply steady
pressure, do not massage.* With the right hand, take hold of the top of
the foot and rotate it.

Commentary: Use the same care with sore spots as you did in the last
move. Work with as many sore spots as you find on the outside of the
heel.

   If you cannot easily rotate the foot, move your body to a more comfortable position.

   This move also reflexes the lower pelvic areas, more toward the sides
of the body than Position 6.

POSITION 8 ~ THE TOE PULL

Start with the little toe. Allow the base of the toe to rest over the index finger of your right hand. The thumb is placed slightly below where the toe connects to the foot. Your left hand is placed over the right hand for support. Pull straight back, while lifting and shaking the foot rhythmically a couple of times. The toes may or may not make a cracking sound. Do each toe. Be gentle.*

*FOOTNOTE: Do not pull on the toes if the person has arthritis there, or has severe back problems.

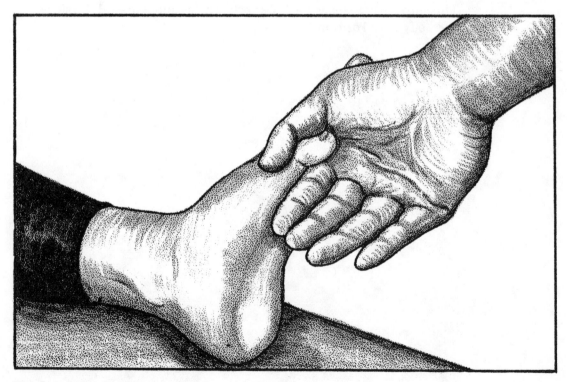

Hand positions for the toe pull

Commentary: Hold each toe just tightly enough so it won't slip from your fingers. If it is sweaty, you can use a sock over the toe and then pull it.

Do not be concerned if the toes don't crack. It is the pull that is important. Go a bit easy on the big toe.

As you shake the foot, ripples of energy go through the body. It's a bit like shaking a garden hose. You shake one end, and a wave travels down the hose to the other end. If this move is done properly, it is not painful, and you will see your friend's head move slightly with the shaking.

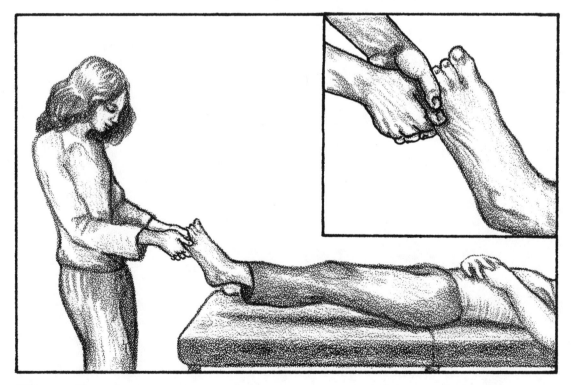

The toe pull.

POSITION 9~KNUCKLE RUBBING
Make a fist with your right hand and deeply massage the entire sole of the right foot with the knuckles of your right hand. Your left hand supports the foot. Work for a while on any sore spots you discover.

Commentary: Encourage your friend to relax as you apply pressure to sore spots. Again, give only as much pressure as your friend can enjoy.

Note the location of any sore spots on the foot, for use in specific moves later on.

Suggestion: Practice LESSON ONE before going on.

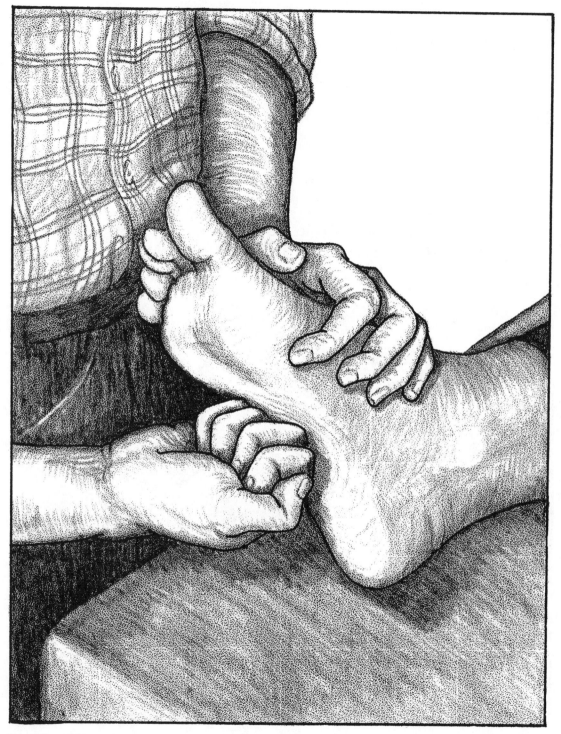

Knuckle rubbing

LESSON TWO

POSITION 10 ~ FLEXED TENDON PRESS

The heel of the left hand pushes back on the ball of the right foot, so that the large tendon under the big toe is flexed. While the tendon is stretched, press down on it with the right thumb. Start at the top of the tendon and go all the way down, pressing deeply. Do this a few times, giving extra attention and pressure to sore spots.

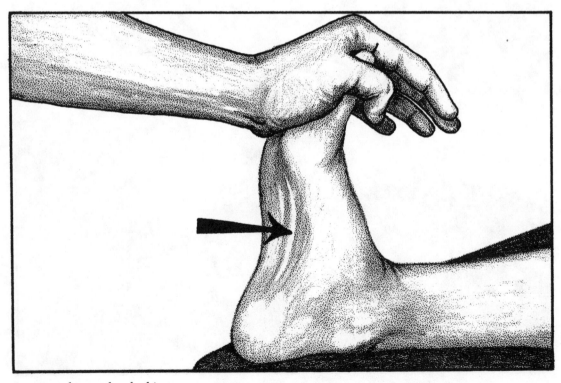

Large tendon under the big toe

Commentary: In this move, the toes are not pressed back; only the ball of the foot is pressed back so that the tendon will be stretched.

A series of rapid presses on the tendon will not be as painful as very slow movements.

If you place the fingers of your right hand over the top of the foot, your thumb will have more leverage and power behind it. If your thumb gets tired or if you want to press deeper, carefully use a knuckle on the sore spots.

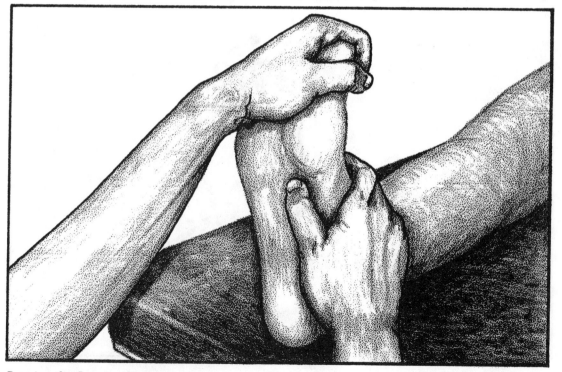

Pressing the flexed tendon.

POSITION 11 ~ CUBOID PRESS, ANKLE ROTATION
Place yourself at a 45–degree angle from the foot. Halfway between the
heel and toes, on the outside of the foot, you will find a little bone. This
is the cuboid bone. Put your thumbs under both sides of this bone. The
rest of your fingers are wrapped over the top of the foot. Press up with
your thumbs while you rotate the ankle.

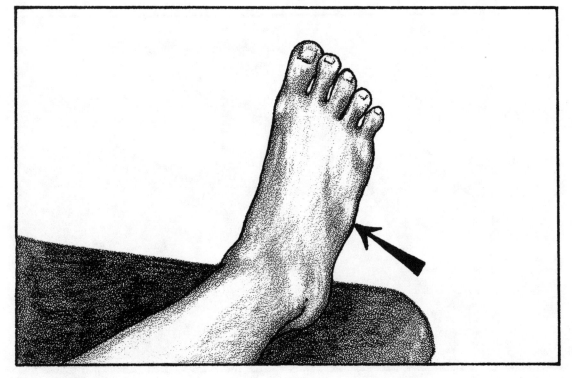

The cuboid bone

Commentary: Adjust your position so you are comfortable as you rotate the ankle.

The work on the feet is basically intended to release blocked energy. Because we are working on the south pole of the body alone, we are not concerned here with polarizing the life-force. *It doesn't matter which hand you use, except for your own comfort. Complete all moves on the person's right foot, then all the moves on the left foot.* If you know reflexology, or any other foot massage, this would be an ideal time to include it.

Suggestion: Stop here and try out what you have just read.

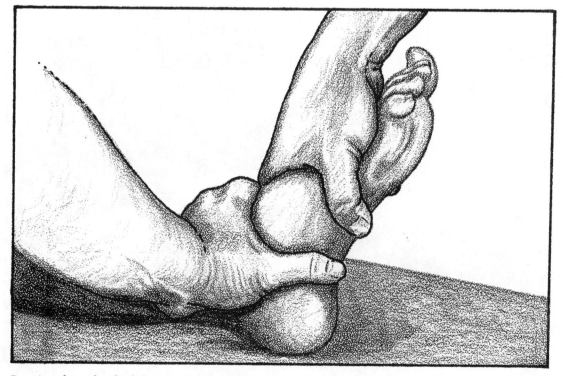

Pressing the cuboid while rotating the ankle.

POSITION 12~RIGHT AND LEFT SIDE OCCIPITAL PRESS
Turn your friend's head to the left so that it is tilted to a 45–degree angle.
Place your left hand so that it is resting across the forehead and is sup-
porting it in that position. The middle finger of the right hand presses
up into the base of the right side of the occipital bone. Maintain pressure for a couple of minutes, then turn the head to do the same move
to the other side with hands reversed.

Middle finger into the base of occipital bone approximately one inch from the
ear.

Commentary: Your middle finger doing the pressing should feel the base of the occipital bone.

No pressure should be applied by the hand that is across the forehead.

For greater strength with the middle finger, use the hand position illustrated.

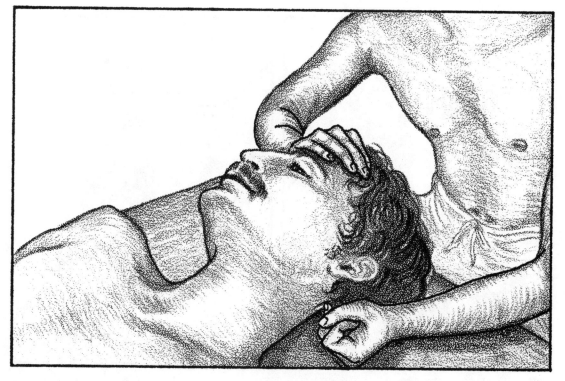

Occipital press — full view

POSITION 13~THUMB WEBBING AND FOREARM STIMULATION

From your friend's right side, take the right hand and squeeze the webbing between the thumb and index finger. Use the thumb and index finger of your right hand and find a sore spot there. With your left hand, apply pressure to find a sore spot just below the elbow toward the outside of the arm. Alternately stimulate the sore areas of the webbing and forearm.

Commentary: To find the sore spot on the forearm, look about one inch below the crease in the elbow, and about an inch from the outside of the arm.

It will be more comfortable for your friend if you place the fingers of your left hand under the elbow to support it while you stimulate the forearm.

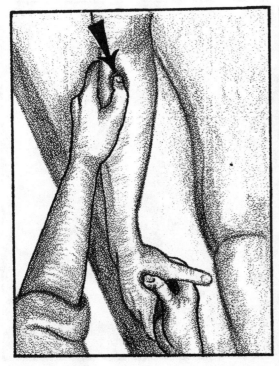

Thumb webbing hold—bottom view   Thumb webbing hold—top view

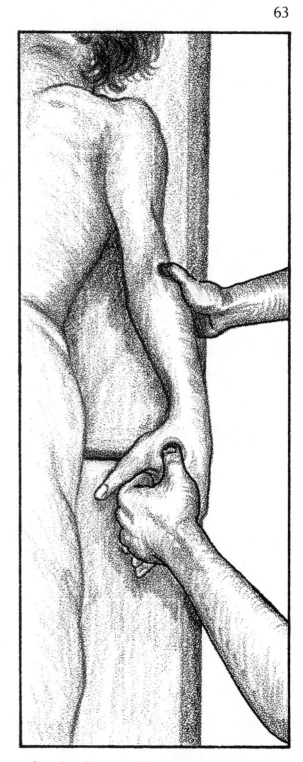

Thumb webbing and forearm stimulation.

POSITION 14~THE FINGER PULL
Take a good solid hold at the base of each finger with your right hand.
Pull the finger until the arm is fully extended off the ground, and push
back on the arm with the left hand. Pull each finger once.

Commentary: This move need only take a few seconds.

Do not be concerned about whether or not the fingers crack, just give
them a good pull.

Now do positions 12, 13, and 14 on your friend's left side.

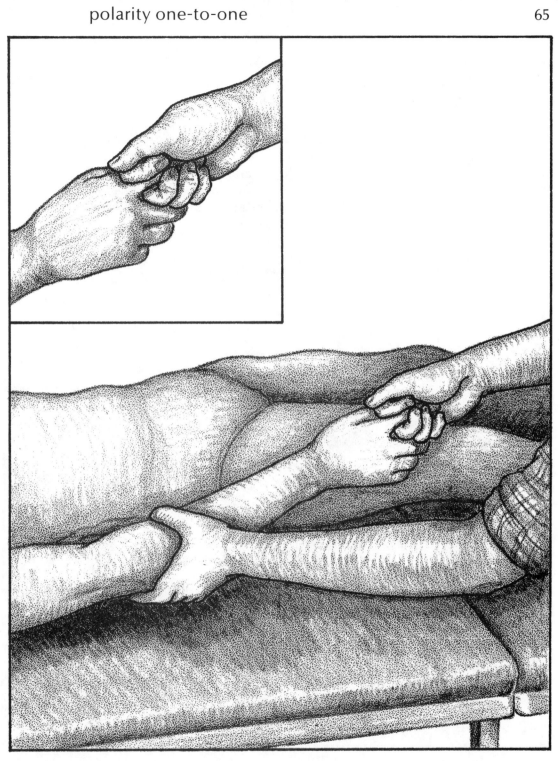

The finger pull

POSITION 15~COLLAR BONE, SOLAR PLEXUS ROCK

From your friend's right side, place the palm of your right hand on the solar plexus, just under the center of the rib cage. Your left hand forms a fist, with the thumb pointing downward. Press your thumb on the underside of your friend's collar bone. Now rock with both hands. Gradually move your left thumb along the entire area under the collar bone on both the left and right sides. Because your left hand is above and your right is below in the center of the body, your left hand is free to work both right and left collar bones, and can still polarize the energy.

Collar bone ridge

Commentary: Most of the pressure and rocking is done with the left hand.

As you rock, hold your left thumb steady so it doesn't slide around on the collar bone.

When you come to sore spots on the underside of the collar bone, you can work them a bit longer. After you have worked a very sore spot there, stop the rocking and leave your hands in place, and feel the life-force surging between your hands.

Suggestion: Practice LESSON TWO before going on.

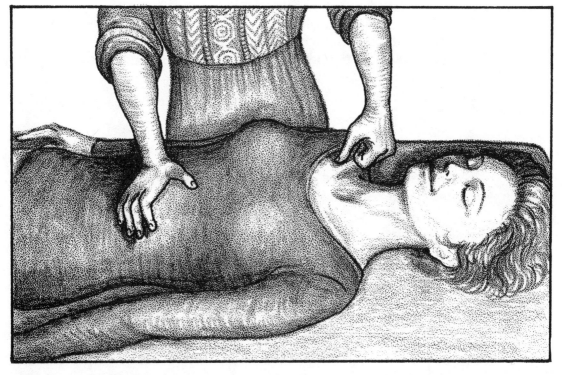

Collar bone solar plexus rock

LESSON THREE

Finishing Moves

Now that the deep release work has freed blocked life-force, we will use subtle touch techniques to polarize the energy. Rub your hands together briskly before each move, and throw off static energy after each move, shaking your hands as though you were throwing off water.

POSITION 16~HAND AND FOOT
From the right side, your right hand holds the person's left foot, and your left hand holds the person's right hand.

From the left side, your left hand holds the person's right foot, and your right hand holds the person's left hand.

Commentary: Before you start, rub your hands vigorously together.
Leave your hands in place as long as you feel any tingling energy in them.

Is your friend still breathing deeply?

This position is the same as Positions 5 and 6 of the polarity circle.

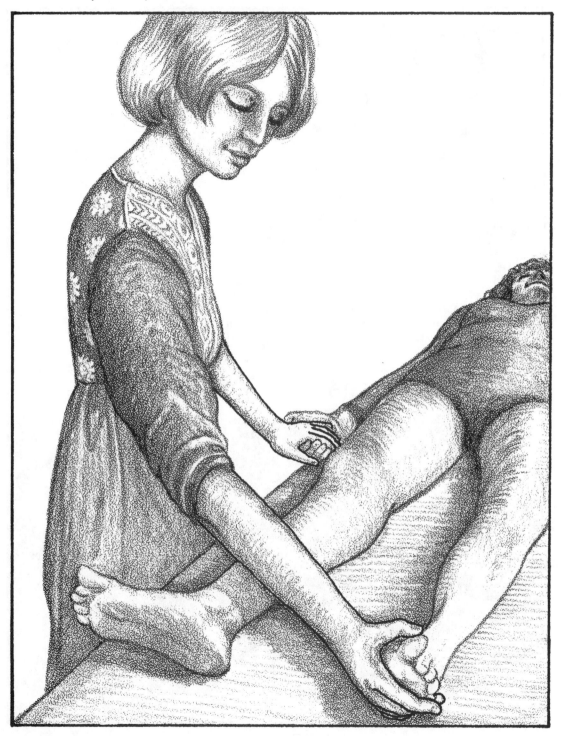

Hand and foot position

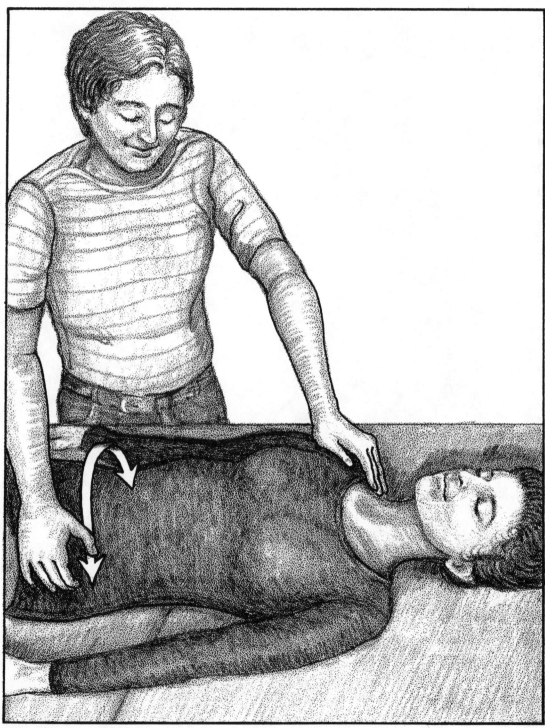

Hip and shoulder hold

POSITION 17~HIP ROCK AND SHOULDER HOLD
Be on the right side of the person. Rest your right hand on the left hip bone, and your left hand on the right shoulder. Rock the hips back and fourth rhythmically for a couple of minutes, then stop. Leave your hands in place while the energy feels strong.

Next, do this same move from the left side of the person. Reverse your hand positions, so your right hand is on the left shoulder, and your left hand is on the right hip.

Commentary: Be sure to rock only the hips and not the shoulders.

When the rocking is stopped, both you and your friend will likely feel a rush of life-force. You will feel it in your hands, and your friend will experience it rushing through the entire body. I usually experience the tingling in my hands from one to five minutes.

This position is the same as Positions 3 and 4 of the polarity circle.

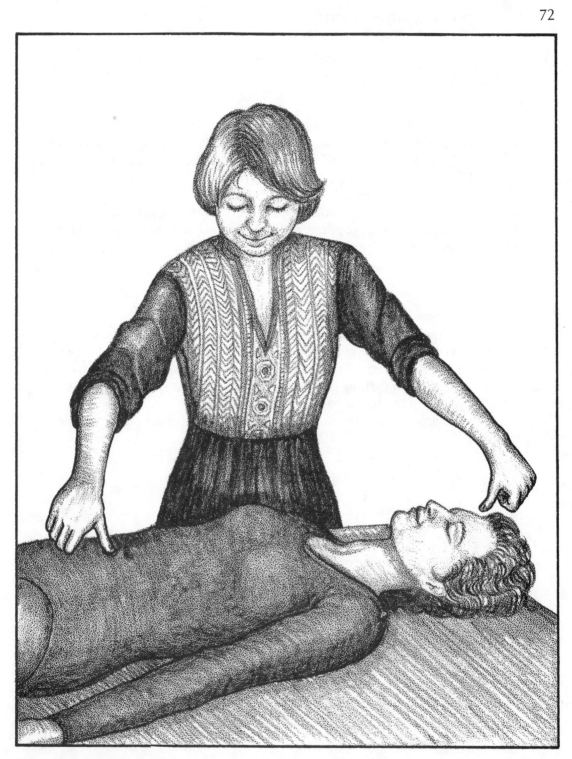

Forehead and navel position

POSITION 18∼FOREHEAD AND NAVEL

From the right side of your friend, make fists with both hands so the thumbs are pointing downward. Gently touch the right thumb to a spot slightly below the navel. The left thumb, also pointing downward, makes no physical contact and is placed in the center of the forehead, about three-fourths inch above the brows. Leave your hands in place a few minutes.

Commentary: Note that the left hand does not touch the forehead. The energy is contacted nicely when the left thumb is about three-fourths inch *off* the forehead. You may experience a sharp tingling in your left thumb. It is not uncommon for people receiving this move to see beautiful colors and go to sleep.

Be as comfortable as you can in this position.

POSITION 19~CROWN SPREAD

Evenly spread your fingers above the forehead, while your thumbs are above the crown of your friend's head. Your thumbs do not touch each other, and there is no physical contact on this move.

Commentary: Assume a comfortable position.

This is a very relaxing and powerful move. Leave your hands in place as long as you feel a strong energy exchange.

Remember to rub your hands together before you start and to throw off the static energy when you finish.

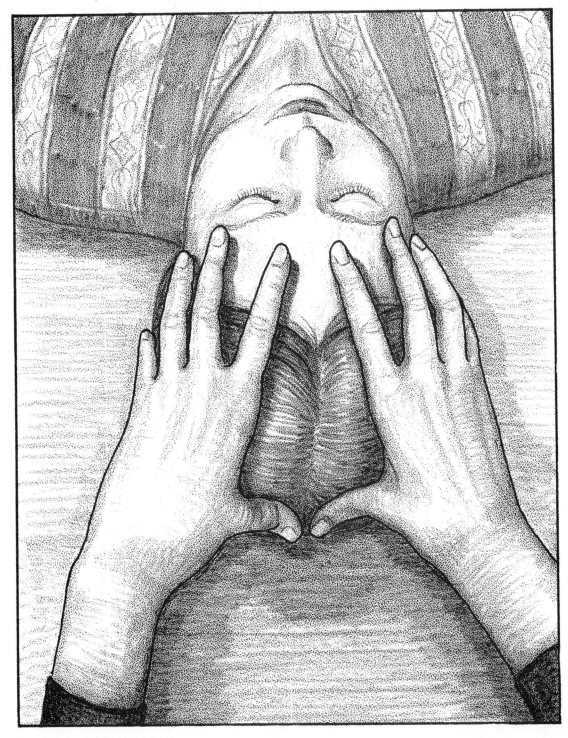

Crown spread

POSITION 20~SPINAL CHARGING

Have your friend roll over onto his or her stomach. Rub your hands together vigorously, then place your right hand on the base of his or her spine, and your left hand at the bottom of the neck. Rock gently with your right hand a few minutes, then leave your hands in place as long as you feel the life-force.

Commentary: This move is especially important in this series if your friend has back problems.

Rock in the same manner as in the tummy rock. After a minute or two with your hands in position, lift them slightly above the person's back and keep them at a level where you feel the greatest charge in your hands.

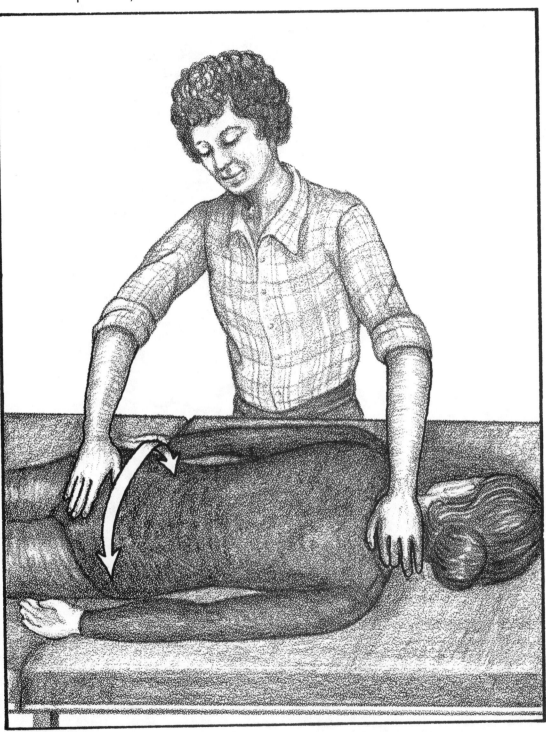

Spinal charging

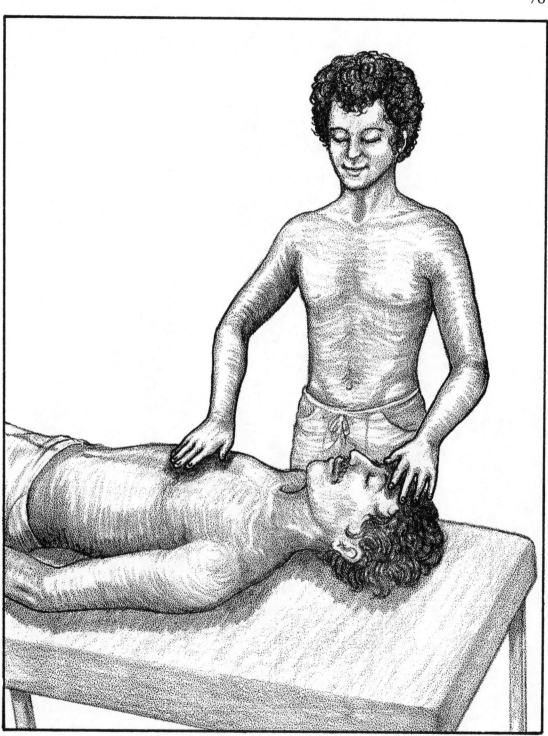

Center charging

POSITION 21 ~ CENTER CHARGING

Have your friend roll over onto his or her back. Rub your hand together vigorously, and when you feel a strong charge in your hands, place your right hand over the heart an inch or two above the body and your left hand slightly above the forehead. Hold this position as long as the life-force exchange feels strong.

Commentary: Keep your hands at a level where you feel the strongest charge of life-force in your hands.

Let your friend rest as long as she or he wants. This is a good time to rinse off your hands in cold water. When you get a sense that your friend is ready, proceed with Positions 22 and 23.

POSITION 22~BACK BRUSH OFF

Help your friend sit up when you feel he or she is ready. Gently stroke the back with your fingers in the following pattern: Start with your right hand on the right shoulder, and your left hand on the left shoulder. Brush across the back so the hands cross at the bottom of the neck and continue to the shoulders. Now, bring your right hand down the left side of the body while your left is going down the right side. Your hands cross over again below the waist. Do this about ten times.

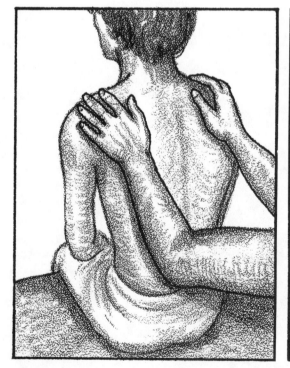

1–Starting position

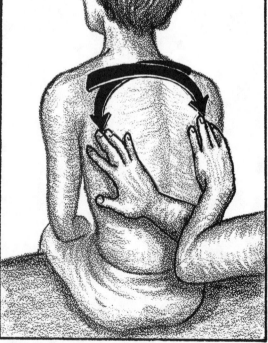

2–Hands cross at the neck

Commentary: Start with a firm stroke and get lighter and lighter each time, until you are barely touching. Continue doing the move without touching.

Throw off static energy each time you brush off.

This is a good move you can do on friends when you have only a few minutes.

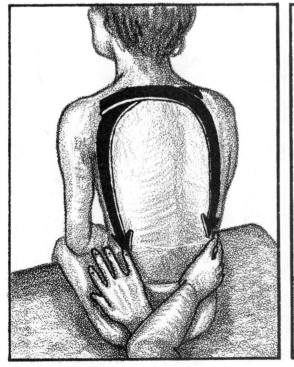

3–Down the sides

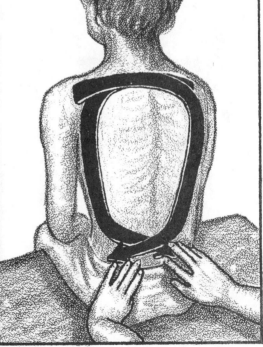

4–Hands cross at base of spine.

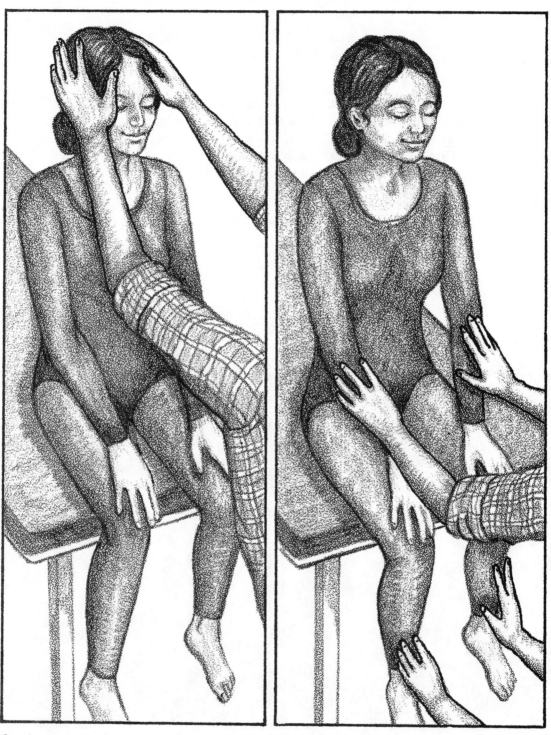

Starting position

Brushing off front

POSITION 23~FRONT BRUSH OFF
Brush from the front, starting from the top of the head. Your right hand
will go down the left side and your left hand will go down the right side
of your friend. Do this about ten times.

Commentary: Use the same touching techniques as in the previous
move.

At this point, allow your friend to rest as long as he or she pleases.
*Rinse your hands in cool water again to remove any static energy. Be
sure to give your friend a glass of water, juice or herbal tea.*
I recommend that you practice the three lessons of the general polarity
session before going on to the specific moves. Specific moves work best in
conjunction with the general polarity session.

Simplicity

There has long been a popular assumption that good medicine has to be bitter, that a treatment should be painful to be effective, and that an intelligent system must be complicated. Polarity energy balancing breaks this tradition because it is simple yet effective. Don't be deceived by the simplicity of the system. While it may appear to be as simple as an apple on a tree, polarity is as mysterious as the very life within a cell. The polarity system, a method of restoring the natural flow of life-force, provides new tools for healing and personal transformation, and could easily create a revolutionary impact in health consciousness.

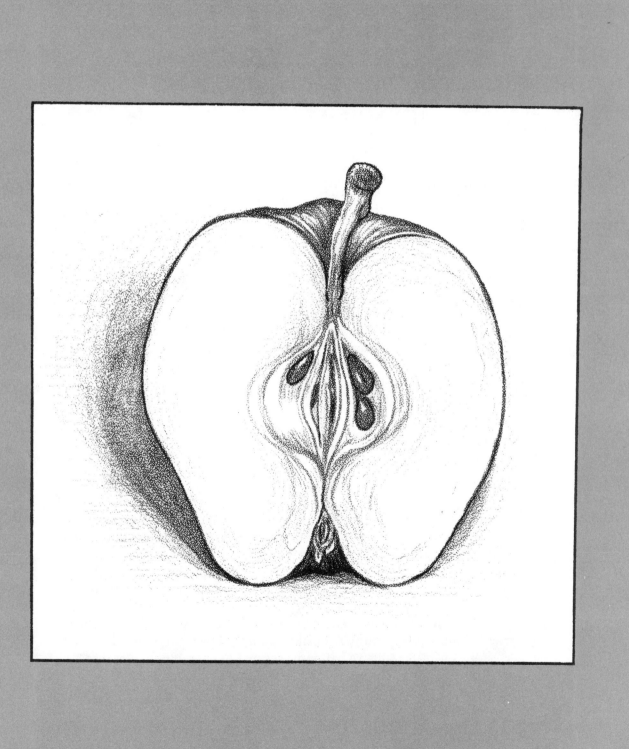

SECTION III

Specific Moves

After you have mastered the general polarity session, you are ready to start specific moves. The general polarity session is excellent for getting life-force moving through the body and breaking up static energy patterns. Specific moves are designed to concentrate the flow of life-force through those parts of the body which express the most blockage. *Use specific moves after Position 15, which is before the finishing moves of the general one-to-one session.*

Reflexive Harmonics

In our day-to-day living, we tend to think that science has things pretty well figured out. We forget that the most basic forces in our lives are as yet unexplainable mysteries. For example, we don't know the fundamental scientific basis for magnetism, gravity or even electricity—nor do we need to know in order to make effective use of them. Life-force is as great a mystery as magnetism, gravity or electricity. In the same way that we have learned to use these forces, we can learn to use the life-force, our most readily available natural resource.

Each cell in the body is a reflection of the whole body and contains the genetic information required to make a complete body. In some related sense, an intricate reflexive harmonic action links specific areas of the

anatomy.* The body seems to have an invisible communication
network. This is what Randolph Stone called the 'Wireless Anatomy'. As
in the case of magnetism, you don't need to understand why it's there in
order to use it. Let's examine how this applies to specific moves.

Our bodies can be divided horizontally into electrically positive(+),
neutral (O), and negatively (—) charged zones. Positively charged zones
harmonically reflect the condition of other positively charged zones.
The same is true for negative and neutrally charged zones. The applica-
tion of pressure stimulation or introduction of life-force into a positive,
negative, or neutral zone will be transmitted and harmonically reflexed
into other similarly charged zones.

Horizontal Polarity Zones

Every portion of the body can be divided horizontally into positive, neutral and negatively charged zones. The area from the shoulders to the
top of the head can be split into positive, neutral and negatively charged
zones. The regions from the pelvis to the shoulders and from the feet to
the hips can be classified in the same manner. The palms of the hands
and the soles of the feet are also sectioned into the same three zones.

*Positively charged zones harmonically reflex other positively charged
zones. The same is true for negatively and neutrally charged zones.*

Center Line

The body can also be divided vertically. We can draw a straight line from
the nose to the belly button, and call this the center line of the body. If
you stand with your feet together, you will see that your big toes are close
to the center line of your body, while the little toes are toward the outside of the body. The big toes will reflex to areas near the center line of
the body, whereas the smaller toes reflex to areas farther away from
the center line.

*FOOTNOTE: Reflex—pertaining to an involuntary response to stimulus; Reflect—to cast
back an image.

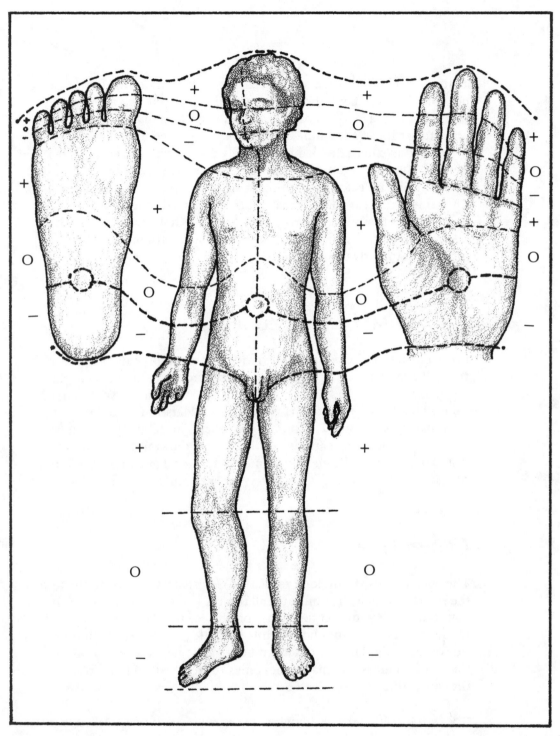

Polarity Zone Chart

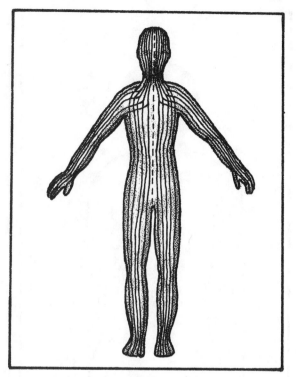

Center-line of the body

Locating Sore Spots—Principles

PRINCIPLE 1: *Sore spots will be found in corresponding locations of like-charged zones.*

You can use the vertical and horizontal zones to formulate specific moves. Let's say that while massaging your friend's foot, you found a sore spot on the place marked x on the foot. This place is two-thirds of the way up the positively charged section of the foot, close to the center line of the body. Now we look across to the chest which also has a positive charge, and we mark an x two-thirds of the way up near the center line of the body. If you investigate this area, you will probably find a very sore spot on the chest as well. There will be a very sore spot on the leg two-thirds of the way up in the positive zone, toward the center line, and a spot on the forehead, as well as on the hand. All the spots marked x are likely to be sore.

PRINCIPLE 2: *What is true for the left side is often true for the right side.*

When you find a sore spot on the left side of the body, you will prob-

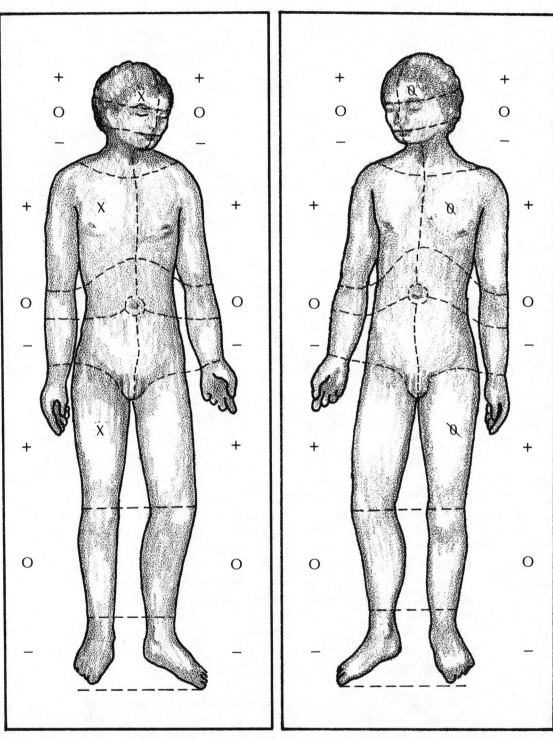

"X" marks the sore spots in corresponding locations of like-charged zones.

"Q" marks the sore spots mirrored on the left side of the body.

ably find another sore spot on the right side of the body. All of the lo-cations marked ϕ correspond to places that will be sore on the left side, reflexing those sore spots already found on the right side of the body.

PRINCIPLE 3: *What is true for the front is often true for the back*.
     When you find a sore spot on the front of the person, you will probably find another sore spot on the back of the person.

PRINCIPLE 4: *Sore spots will often be found around the major joints of the body*.
     The major joints are the ankles, knees, hips, wrists, elbows, shoulders, and neck. Major joints are like intersections for the life-force and often become congested. You can usually find sensitive areas near these major joints.

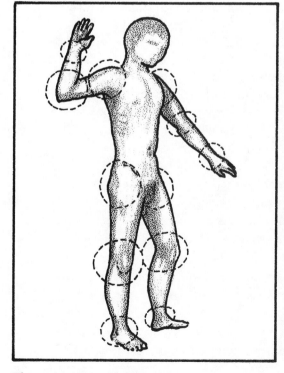

The major joints of the body

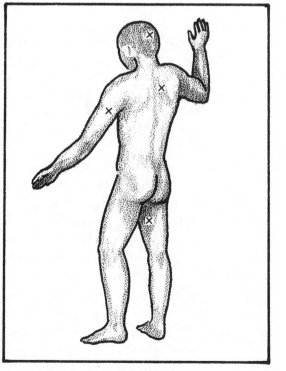

Reflex points on the back side

Identifying the Sore Spots

Sore spots are often related to imbalances in tissue, muscles, bones, organs, blood, and lymph. By looking at a physiology chart of the organs, you can see their locations on the body, and can associate them with corresponding sore places. For example, to find where the liver reflexes, look at a physiology chart and you will see that the liver is on the right side of the body just behind the lower part of the rib cage. Look at it in relation to the center line of the body. Note that its location is at the bottom of the positively charged zone of the chest. Now look at the foot chart, and you can clearly see why the liver reflexes to that part of the foot.

You can find spots where the life-force is blocked, and know that something is going on in that area. Unless you are a licensed physician, you do not have enough information to say any more than that. Avoid suggesting diagnoses at all times.

When someone is in a weakened condition, they may be highly susceptible to suggestion. It is hazardous to tell someone what you think is wrong with them. They might believe you. Some people are waiting for an opportunity to jump onto some symptom and magnify it into a full-blown disease or disability. The suggestion of illness may make a person worry and the belief that one is sick may go a long way in creating ill health.*

*FOOTNOTE: The way the laws stand in all fifty states, you must not claim that you treat, diagnose, prescribe, or give healing therapy. People with illness, under law, must be informed that they should consult a licensed medical practitioner in the necessary field. You can recommend that they see a doctor who is involved in holistic health practices, such as a naturopathic doctor, a chiropractor, or osteopath who is experienced in nutritional therapy and fasting. A good suggestion is to write the American Holistic Medical Association, Route 2, Welch Coulee, La Crosse, Wisconsin 54601 for a recommendation of someone in your area.

You can give polarity sessions for educational, recreational, or research purposes, or as part of your religion. For legal reasons, make no claims that you will treat, diagnose, prescribe, give therapy, or heal.

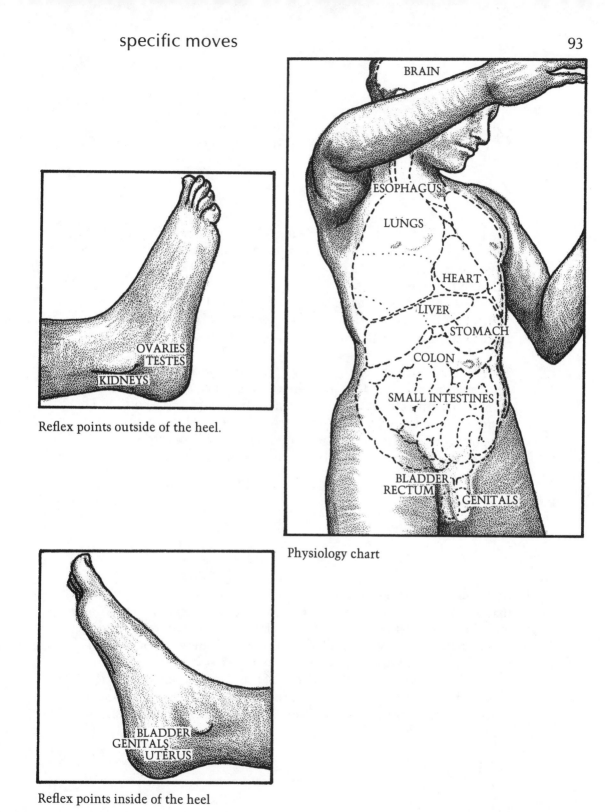

Reflex points outside of the heel.

Physiology chart

Reflex points inside of the heel

The Principles for Specific Moves

The key principle to remember when applying specific moves is to find the sore spots on one or both sides of the blockage, and polarize the energy through it.

This is how it is done:

1. *Determine where the blockage of life-force occurs.*

First find a sore spot on the foot, then look at the Polarity Zone Chart and determine which organ or general area of the body it reflexes.

2. *Plan to polarize the energy along vertical or diagonal lines of force.*

If you think of the body as being like a bar magnet, you will see that there is a positive charge on top, and a negative charge at the bottom. The greatest difference in polar charges is from the top to the bottom. You can polarize the energy along the centerline vertically or across the body diagonally with success. Horizontal lines of current are not as effective.

Caution: Do not press on spots that are injured or infected. This means that if someone has a broken wrist or an infection, you don't press down on it. You can however, do three things. First, you can give the person the general polarity session. Second, you can channel energy through sensitive places without touching them. Third, if a wrist is broken, you can deeply massage the other uninjured wrist because they reflex each other. Also, do not press deeply into internal organs, i.e. large intestines, small intestines, bladder, etc. Apply pressure only on muscle tissue and against bones.

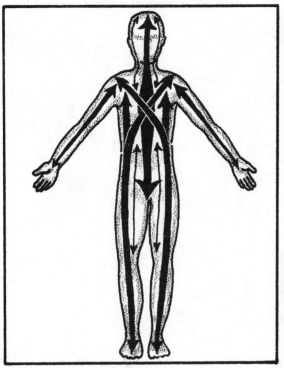

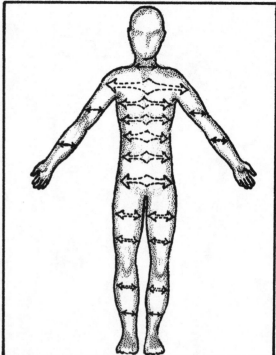

Strong lines of force   Weak lines of force

Applying the Principles

Let us see how we can apply all the principles of specific moves.

1. *Identify sore spots with their corresponding organs or areas of the body.*

We start while massaging the feet. Pay attention to any sore spots on the feet. Note where they are, and what other areas they reflex. As an example, let's say that we find a sore point in the upper part of the neutral zone on the sole of one of the feet. Look at the chart and you will see that this spot reflexes to the area of the transverse colon.

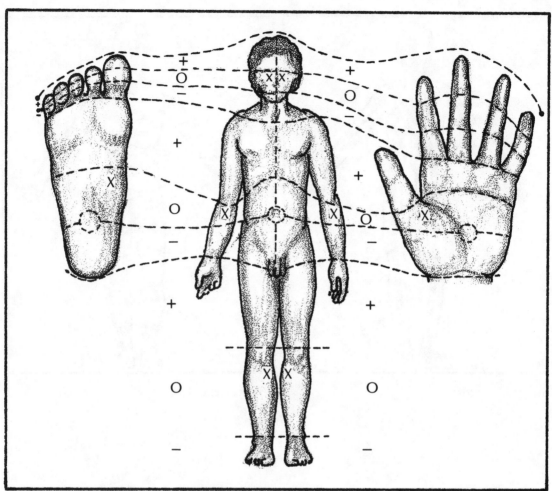

Sore spots reflexing the transverse colon.

2. *Identify and locate the corresponding reflex sore spots.*

Corresponding sore spots in our example will be on the other foot, and on the calves in the upper part of the neutral zone of the lower leg. Next, you may likely find sore spots on the palm of the hand toward the upper part of the neutral zone. Likewise, a sore spot might be found in the upper part of the neutral zone of the forearm. Check for sore spots on the cheek bones and on the back. All of these areas are likely to have sore spots.

3. *Polarize sore spots to unblock the life-force.*

You can be very creative channeling the energy between the sore spots. Here are some of the possible variations:

- Your right hand holds the reflexive sore spot on the left foot, and your left hand holds the intestinal reflexive sore spot on the right hand.

  On this move there is a good cross current that will move through the leg, through the entire torso including the intestine, up to the shoulder, and down to the hand. Next, do it from the other side to keep both sides balanced. *Work the left and right sides of the body equally to keep the life-force balanced.*
- Your right hand holds the sore spot on the sole of the left foot, and your left hand holds the sore spot on your friend's right forearm. This is similar to the last move, and is valuable for the same reasons. This position opens up another important reflex center.
- Another variation would be for the person to lay on his or her stomach, with the knees bent so the feet are up in the air. Your right hand stimulates the sore spots on either the left or right foot while your left hand works reflexive sore spots along the underside of the cheek bone.

  This is working the long currents of the body. They are called long currents because they span long distances. Short current moves are beneficial in a small area, while long current moves have a more general benefit over the entire body. It's a good idea while you are creating specific moves to include both long and short current moves.
- Your friend is lying on his or her back. Hold your left hand over the intestines (use no pressure), and with your right hand, locate and stimulate sore places on the calves. Give as much pressure to the calf as your friend can accept. (*Note:* your left hand is above in the center of the body, so your right hand is free to polarize both left and right sides.)

  Your left hand is not applying pressure, so be sure to rub your hands together before making contact with the energy field of the person. When you finish with any non-pressure moves, be sure to shake your hands to remove static energy.

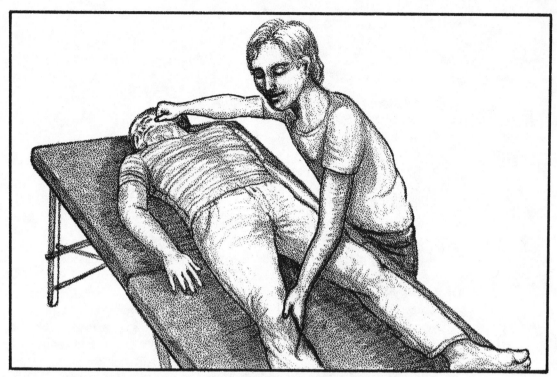

Polarizing reflexive sore spots on the cheek and calf.

- Stimulate the sore spots on the left side of the cheek bone with your right hand, while your left hand contacts the sore spots on the right leg below the knee. After you finish this, be sure to do the other side of the body to keep both sides balanced.

Each of the above variations channels energy through important reflexive centers for the intestines.

4. *Channel between sore spots of different origins.*
If you find sore spots related to other organs, or areas of the body, you can work any two unrelated points with each other. See that the currents of energy are going through the parts of the body that express the most blockage.

For example, you could polarize the intestinal reflex point of the calves with the lung reflex points of the chest.

The main idea is to work the sore spots and polarize the energy through the places that express the most blockage.

Summary

Any time that your hands are polarizing the life-force through areas expressing blockage, the move will be of benefit.

The basic ways to channel life-force for specific moves are:

1. Find and work reflex points above and below the area expressing blockage.

2. Find and work a reflex point above the blockage, while you channel directly into the blocked area with your other hand using no pressure.

3. With one hand find and work a reflex point below the point of blockage, while the other hand channels directly into the blockage.

4. Work two reflex points together that are not directly in the path of the blockage.

5. Combine unrelated reflex points that are above and below the areas of blockage.

Dynamic Centers

There are certain centers of the body that are highly receptive to the flow of life-force. These centers can be used along with any other sore reflex point.
   These centers are:
   *   The coccyx
   *   The navel
   *   The base of the occipital bone

The Coccyx

The coccyx (tip of the tail bone) is one of the most important polarity centers. Its value cannot be overemphasized. Because of its location at the very end of the spine, the coccyx has the maximum negative polarity of any point in the spine. You can put the middle finger of your right hand* on the very tip of the tail bone, and connect your left hand to any other sore spot above the coccyx. This move is wonderful for back problems, easing child birth, relaxing tension-related illness, and is a great addition to your general sessions.

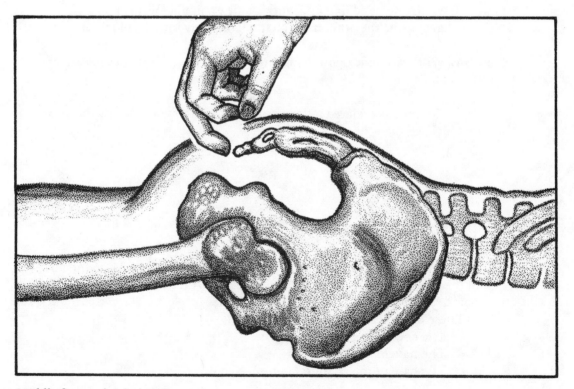

Middle finger of right hand on coccyx.

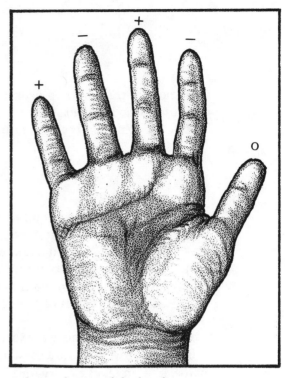

Polarity charges of the hand

*FOOTNOTE: Each of your fingers has a charge.

   The little finger has a positive charge.

   The ring finger has a negative charge.

   The middle finger has a positive charge.

   The index finger has a negative charge.

   The thumb has a neutral charge.

   You can send the maximum positively charged current through a negative zone, such as the coccyx, by using the middle finger of the right hand. Likewise, use the index finger of the left hand when you are working a maximum positively charged zone, like the forehead. For more theory, refer to Dr. Stone's books.

Do not use this point on people who have very high blood pressure, or on those prone to epilepsy.

Here are some good general moves you can do using the coccyx:

POSITION 1: Have your friend lie on his or her left side. The tip of the middle finger of your right hand gently stimulates and massages the very tip of the coccyx. You can use a soft vibrating massage with your right hand. Your left hand rests at the back of the neck. Rock the person very gently, using the palms of your hands. You can rock a long time and then stop, leaving your hands in place for as long as you feel the life-force.

Commentary: This move is excellent for relieving tension in the spine. It is a good move to include as a part of your general session. For back pains, it often takes twenty-four hours for the full results to become apparent.

In order to get to the tip of the coccyx, it is necessary for the person receiving the polarity to partially undress. The maximum benefit is obtained from the coccyx move if the middle finger is right at the tip of the coccyx. Because the coccyx is near the anus, many people like to wrap tissue around their finger for sanitary reasons.

Soreness at this point is common, so be very gentle at first.

POSITION 2: With your friend lying on his or her stomach, the middle finger of your right hand connects to the tip of the coccyx. Let the rest of the right hand cover part of the buttocks. Your left hand can be stimulating sore reflex points on the back. Rock with the right hand.

Commentary: You will often find sore reflex points about three-fourths inch on either side of the spine. Press on these spots using the thumb and index fingers of your left hand.

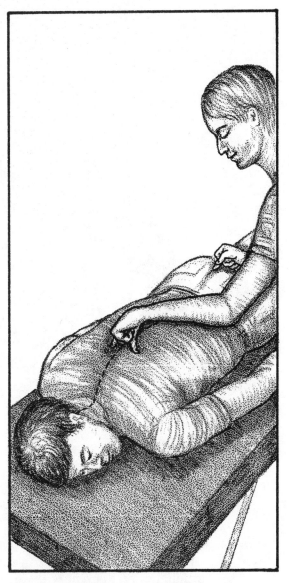

Polarizing life-force through the spine.

Rock in a gentle rhythmical way as in other rocking moves. When you stop the rocking, leave your hands in place as long as you feel the exchange of life-force in your hands.

This move helps relieve back tension and balances the corresponding reflexive organs.

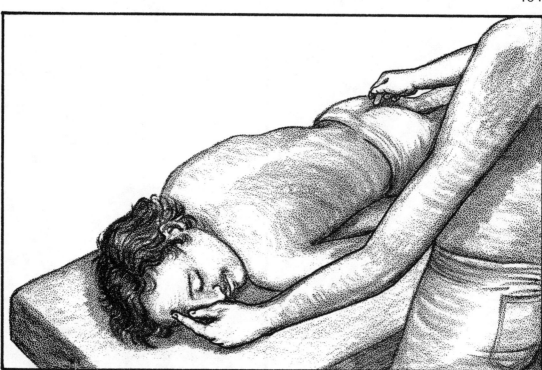

Polarizing energy between coccyx and brow center.

POSITION 3: Again, place your right middle finger at the tip of the coccyx, and your left hand can stimulate the sore places around the occipital ridge. Rocking with your right hand is optional.

Commentary: Here we are linking two dynamic centers together, which creates a very powerful effect. This move is good for balancing the life force through the spine and all reflexing organs. Any time your hands are sending energy through the spine like this, it will be helpful for back pains.

 If you rock the body on this move, rock only with the palm of the right hand.

POSITION 4: Be on the left side of your friend, who is on his or her stomach, head facing to the left. Touch the middle finger of your right hand to the tip of the coccyx, and have your left index finger make energy contact one-half inch away from the center of the forehead.

Commentary: Hold your index finger about one-half inch off the skin with your thumb touching the base of the index finger, and all the other fingers together loosely as if making a fist. This hand position increases the power of channeling through the left hand.

The Navel Center

The navel center is also of particular value. You can connect and polarize this center to numerous sore spots or other key centers of the body. Remember, that *in order to affect any particular organ or area of the body, all that is necessary is to send energy through that part of the body.* The navel is central to the torso and is highly receptive to the flow of life-force.

Here are some examples of general moves using the navel center:

POSITION 1: The person is on his or her back, with the soles of the feet together and knees bent. Your right hand holds the big toes of both feet, while the left hand rests on the navel center.

Commentary: This move sends a strong energy flow to the center of the body and will be valuable for any lower central pelvic disturbances. Hold this move as long as you feel a strong energy exchange in your hands.

POSITION 2: Using your right hand, press on the inside or outside of the heel of either the left or right foot. Your left hand rests on the navel center.

Commentary: This is another excellent move for lower pelvic disturbances. Adjust yourself so that your hand positions will be comfortable.

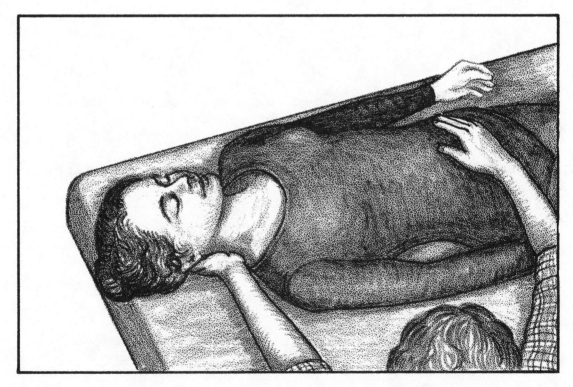

Navel center and back of neck

POSITION 3: Rub your hands together, and place your right hand on the navel center so the thumb rests in the navel (use no pressure). Place your left hand under the back of the neck.

Commentary: This is a very comforting and relaxing move, with general advantage to all the organs between your hands.

POSITION 4: Have your friend lie on his or her left side. From behind the person, place your right middle finger on the coccyx, and your left hand just slightly above the navel center. Apply no pressure.

Commentary: This move is especially good for the pelvic area through which the life-force is being channeled. This position can be extremely beneficial for pregnant women or women in labor, as well as for people with urinary problems or other pelvic disturbances.

The Base of the Occipital Bone

The base of the occipital bone at the top of the spine has a powerful, positive charge. You can use this connective point to bring relaxation to the spine and organs of the body. Connect the base of the occipital bone or even the back of the neck to other sore spots you discover.

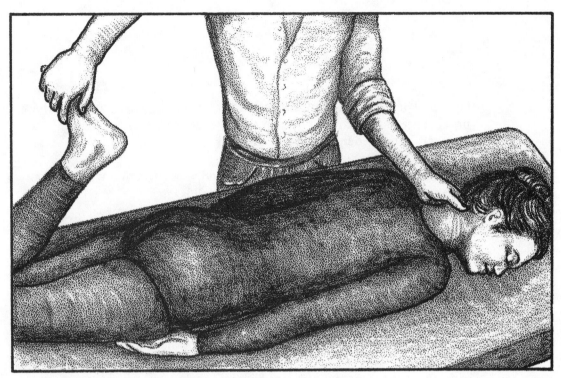

Working the long currents between the feet and occipital bone.

POSITION 1: With your friend on his or her back, rub your hands to-gether, and put your left hand over the occipital bone base at the back of the neck. With your right hand, do a tummy rock.

Commentary: This move is of general advantage to the digestive and respiratory system, as well as the heart and upper back. All the organs between your hands will derive benefit through polarity.

POSITION 2: With your friend on his or her stomach, rest your left hand across the base of the occipital bone. With your right hand, stimulate any sore spots you find on the feet, calves, legs, back or around the major joints of the body.

Commentary: There are many possible ways to channel the energy in a polarized way. Each sore spot, when polarized, releases more blocked energy into the system. The polarized energy will go where it is needed and do what is needed; all you have to do is release the life-force.

POSITION 3: With your friend on his or her stomach, place your left hand over the occipital bone, and with your right hand, find sore spots on the buttocks.

Commentary: If you feel to either side of the genitals, you will find a bony ridge which is the base of the pubis bone. Often there are several sore spots along this ridge. Do not be confused by the large tendon that is just above the pubis bone. It may be more comfortable to work this area with your friend lying on his or her back.

This move is very powerful because you are working a current between a strong positive and a strong negative zone of the body.

Specific Moves Review:

1. Locate the sore spots.
2. Trace their reflexive locations.
3. Work the major sore spots.
4. Polarize them with vertical or diagonal currents.
5. Send energy through those organs and areas of the body that reflex the most blockage.
6. Use the dynamic centers and connect them to specific sore spots.
7. End the polarity with the finishing moves of the general one-to-one session. Be creative, and feel free to use your intuition.
8. Give your friend a large glass of herbal tea, juice, or water after strong sessions.

Remember, a series of sessions is far more valuable than an occasional session.

The life-force in its natural state flows along well-defined pathways. All you have to do is get the energy moving through those areas which reveal the most blockage, and the life-force will do the rest.

Love Is The Best Healer

For centuries, many have said that
love is the best healer.
Love is the power of life-force.
If love becomes blocked,
life-force will become blocked,
and the body will reflect this.
We do not need to try and create love,
for love is our true nature and essence.

SECTION IV

The Polarity Circle

The polarity circle is a new development in the polarity system. It has the advantage of using only non-pressure and non-physical touch techniques, making it totally painless. Children enjoy the polarity circle, and it is so simple to learn that six-year-olds can do it perfectly in just a few minutes. In terms of relief, the circle can be as powerful, or at times, even more powerful than the polarity one-to-one session.

The polarity circle is composed of six people who form a circuit to channel their loving energy into a seventh person. The person who receives the polarity is the center of the circle, and need do nothing but relax, take a few deep breaths, and be willing to experience an increased sense of well-being.

For the comfort of everyone, it helps to use a massage table for the polarity circle, but it can be done on the floor.

The sanskrit sound 'OM' has been known and used in India for thousands of years. I find that this sound has a beneficial harmonizing, vibrating and relaxing effect. During the polarity circle, it is helpful if everyone sings the sound 'OM'. It is pronounced like 'home' without the 'h'. When sung, it is long on the 'O' and short on the 'M' like this, 'OOOOO OOOOOOOOOOOOOOOOOOOOOOOOOOOOMMM'. Its effect seems stronger if everyone can harmonize. The person receiving the polarity need only listen.

Polarity Circle Positions

Person #1 Cradle the head using no pressure. It's best to not quite touch the person, while letting your hands relax. The index and middle fingers go down the sides of the neck, while the thumb rests by the ear. (See p. 38)

Person #2 Be on the right side of the person. Gently rest your left hand on the forehead and place your right hand on the bottom of the rib cage in the center of the body. Use no pressure.

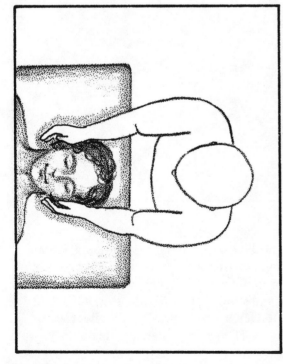

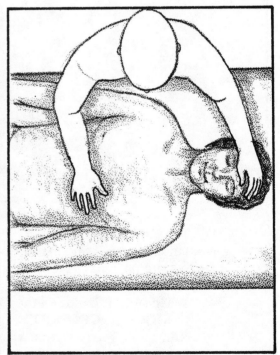

Position 1

Position 2

Person #3 Be on the right side of the person. Rest your right hand on the left hip bone and your left hand on the right shoulder. (See p. 71)

Person #4 Be on the left side of the person. Rest your left hand on the person's right hip bone and your right hand on the left shoulder. (See p. 71)

Person #5 Be on the right side of the person. Your right hand holds the person's left foot and your left hand holds the person's right hand. (See p. 68)

Person #6 Be on the left side of the person. Your left hand holds the right foot, and your right hand holds the person's left hand. (See p. 68)

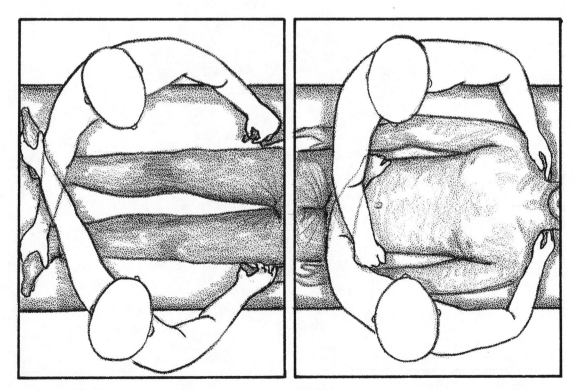

Positions 5 & 6   Positions 3 & 4

The complete polarity circle

Polarity Circle Procedure

1. Tell the person receiving the polarity to relax. Have him take twelve slow, deep breaths, relaxing a little more with each one.

2. When giving the polarity, it's important for everyone to rub their hands vigorously for half a minute. Now hold them a couple of inches away from the hands of the person next to you, with the palms facing each other. When the energy feels strong, proceed.

3. Place hands on indicated positions touching *only* the person receiving the polarity.

4. Those in position numbers three and four will rock the person's hips back and forth rhythmically. Work together to rock gently and evenly. Do not rock the shoulders.

5. Begin to 'OM'. Remember to send your love. Continue from five to fifteen minutes along with the rocking. The longer sessions are often better, so use your own intuition as a guide.

6. Stop 'OMing' and rocking and *leave your hands in place*. Continue sending love. At this point, the energy is likely to be rushing through the person receiving the polarity, while those giving the polarity may feel the energy flowing through their hands. As long as the sensation of energy is strong, everyone should leave their hands in place. When the life-force is no longer felt, it has done its work.

7. Now lift your hands off the person, keeping them from one to six inches above the original positions. Contact the space in which the energy feels the strongest and hold your hands in that position until the energy has nearly dissipated.

8. Take your hands away, and let the person rest as long as he or she likes. Shake your hands as if you were throwing off water, then rinse them in cold water. This grounds and removes static energy. Static energy may be felt as a heaviness or swollen feeling in your hands.

9. Give the person who has received the polarity a large glass of water, juice or herbal tea.

Nature's Integrity

Until man duplicates a blade of grass, Nature can laugh at his so-called scientific knowledge. Remedies from chemicals will never stand in favorable comparison with the products of Nature—the living cell of the plants, the final result of the rays of the sun, the mother of all life.
    —Thomas Edison

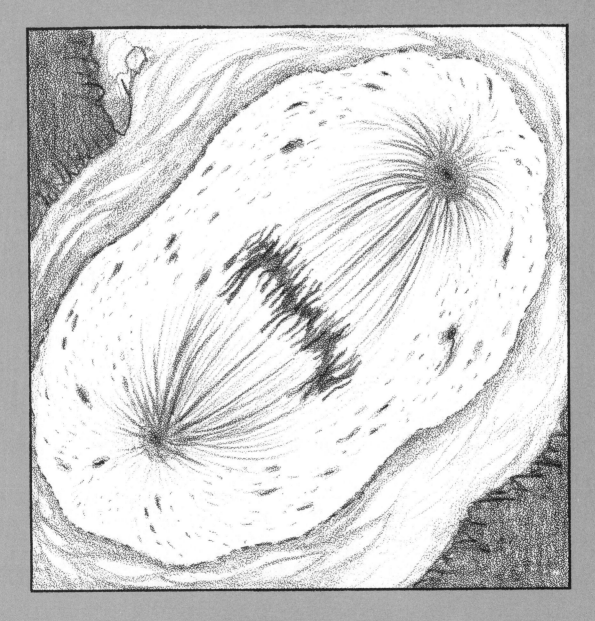

SECTION V

Natural Healing with Life-Force

The Cell

All life is made up of cells. "Each cell of the blood stream, each corpuscle, is a whole universe in itself," wrote Edgar Cayce in his book *Diet and Health*. The human body contains over 100 trillion cells. Each cell has approximately 100,000 different genes. These genes are made of long spiralling chains of DNA which contain the genetically coded blueprint of the whole body. This means that *each* microscopic cell has a genetic map of an entire human body which is comprised of 100,000,000,000,000 living, reproducing and self-healing cells.

These DNA molecules are so incredibly narrow and tightly coiled that if they were all unwound, joined together and stretched out, they would cover a distance of 74 billion, 320 million miles. That's long enough to go all the way from the earth to the sun and back again 400 times. Yet all this DNA can fit into a space the size of an ice cube.

Every moment there are thousands of changes going on at the molecular level within every cell. Many of these events take place within a thousandth of a second.

To attempt to understand the complexity and intricate precision of a single cell is humbling to the intellect.

I suggest that you stop and think about this for a little while.

Modern Medicine and Holistic Health Consciousness

Modern medicine is the science and art of diagnosing and treating diseases. Over 50,000 maladies have been recorded. To know everything about sickness, you would study disease.

Holistic health care is based upon the study of health and wholeness. The holistic view is that when all parts of the person—body, intellect, emotions, and spirit—are balanced, then the person is expressing full health. To know everything about health, you would study healthy people. The attention of the holistic healer is focused on preventative care, natural treatments, and the personal responsibility of each person for his or her own health.

When someone has a cold, the typical question asked is: "How do you stop the uncomfortable symptoms?" Symptoms signal an out-of-balance condition and express the body's attempt to right itself. *The supression of symptoms can be a superficial or dangerous 'cure', by treating the effects and bypassing the true cause.* How about asking this: "Why has the body chosen to eliminate mucous or have a fever? How can we restore the cells to health?" *The body's infinite complexity expresses a wisdom beyond intellectual understanding.*

Drugs can only chemically stimulate or suppress the action of cells. Our knowledge of drugs is based on empirical evidence; that is, by trial and observation of each drug's effect. *Drugs do not heal people, only the cell is capable of healing itself.* The best we can do is to respect the wisdom of the cell. If we create the right environment for our cells, they will heal themselves.

In all fairness, modern medicine deserves great respect. It has achieved tremendous success helping people in times of crisis. In instances of congenital defects, infectious disease, traumatic injury, and many other conditions, allopathic medicine and surgery perform what seem to be miracles.

In the long run however, preventative care is easier, less painful, less expensive and far more effective than crisis work.

Let Us Agree

It is the nature of the body to heal itself. The impulse of self-preservation is biologically very strong, and the human body will do everything possible to maintain and heal itself.

Health and healing must take place on a cellular level. In order to have healthy tissue, you must have healthy cells.

Cells will heal and regenerate quickly if given a favorable environment. Just as a plant needs sunlight, good soil, and water, our cells have special requirements.

A favorable environment for our cells is provided by:
- high quality thoughts and feelings
- high quality food
- regular vigorous exercise

The Quality of Thoughts and Feelings

Polarity is an effective method of recharging the life-force to balance our physical and emotional states. Keeping healthy, however, requires more. To get long lasting results, we must also deal with the causes of imbalances—which can often be traced back to work conditions, personal relationships or lifestyle. Relaxing a tense person is beneficial. But to be healed, that person must also correct the causes of the disturbance.

First in importance is our emotional balance. Our thoughts and feelings affect our health. Psychosomatic medicine has shown that most illnesses are mentally self-induced. During emotional trauma, it is common for people to get sick. Elderly married partners often die one right after the other. After retiring from their jobs, people who do not find some new meaningful activity become bored and depressed, and may even die of some illness. On the other hand, did you ever notice how people 'come alive' when they are feeling lots of love? Physical ailments disappear, the complexion brightens up, reflecting lighter feelings inside. When people are happy and excited the r chances of getting sick are very slim. Attitudes and emotions affect not only your personal health, but also the length of your lifetime. Therefore, it is necessary to cultivate the highest quality attitudes and emotions.

The question arises: "Why does emotional stress adversely affect our health?" First, let us understand that our thoughts bring on definite physical changes in our cells. This is because *the effects of our every thought and feeling resonate within each cell.* Illness caused by the mind is a physical reality.

Love is the power of life-force. Being in love is often said to make a person feel all tingly and bubbly inside. This tingling feeling of exhilaration is a state of openness in which the life-force surges freely through the body. Love is claimed to be the best healer. *If love becomes blocked, life-force will become blocked, and the body will reflect this.* Positive and relaxed thoughts allow the maximum flow of life-force to circulate, resulting in increased health, energy and happiness. Feelings of depression or hate obstruct the flow of life-force. *Whether your thoughts and feelings are of love, hate, the past, present, future, other people or yourself, your cells will personally experience the resulting resonating vibratory quality, and this will directly affect your well-being.*

We naturally believe that what our mind tells us is true. However, the mind's messages are often colored by the conditioning we receive while growing up. We have the ability to overcome this conditioning if we choose to exercise our will. There are many tools to help us. Here are some pointers that I have found to be useful.

POSITIVE THOUGHTS: Pay attention to your every thought as you would to a television program. You don't buy everything you see on the screen, so there is no need to buy everything which crosses your mind. The way we feel about ourselves dynamically shapes our lives, and our beliefs will structure our reality. If a man believes that he is attractive and deserving of love, he will project this, and people will confirm it for him. Likewise, the opposite is true. You do not have to identify or feel victimized by worn-out thought patterns. *You can choose your thoughts. Ask yourself,*

"Does this thought bring me love and harmony?" If it does, that's great. If it does not, recognize that thoughts can serve by teaching you more about yourself—including what needs to be changed.

The more you identify with a thought, the more power it has and the more attached to it you become. Say, for example, a thought comes in your mind and says, "I am unattractive". If you believe this thought you could attach a 100-volt charge of disappointment to it. An alternate way of handling the negativity is to let yourself experience thankfulness and say: "Thank you, thought, for showing me what I have been trained to believe. Thank you for protecting me from frightening social situations in the past. Thank you for helping me know what it's like not to love myself so I can now have more understanding, love, and forgiveness of myself and others. However, I no longer need you. Thank you and good-bye." *Thankfulness is the antidote for stress.*

By no longer identifying with a particular thought, you can more easily let go of it. Disbelieve the negative pictures that you have about yourself. They are only true if you believe that they are. *You* are not the thoughts that you have, because *you* have the power to keep a thought or let go of it. Don't be a slave to your conditioning and early training. Consciously create positive thinking. Soon your positive thoughts will be more real than your negative ones. The difficulties that we experience today help us grow, for they teach us compassion and forgiveness. Our difficulties offer us a precious opportunity—to choose again to love.

We can take charge of our lives by daring to tune in to a positive station in our minds. We can take the point of view that we already love ourselves, and always will, unconditionally. We love who we are, where we are, who we are with, and what we are doing. You become what you think, so why not experience yourself as courageous, inspired, successful, happy, healthy, and loving? Consciously and actively, create positive thoughts. Life is not hard, it is challenging. There are no mistakes or problems, only opportunities to learn. Being positive is a choice, and we have the power to see every situation as a learning experience contributing to our personal growth.

POSITIVE SPEECH: The spoken word is often more powerful than thought. Listen to what you and others say. With practice, you can create totally positive speech to go along with positive thoughts and attitudes.

POSITIVE COMPANY: The people we interact with have an important influence in our lives. To test this for yourself, just watch how you change around very positive, or very negative people. It is our choice if we want to be positive, inspired, excited and joyful—and it is also our choice whether we keep company with people who reinforce or inhibit those qualities in us.

POSITIVE ENVIRONMENT: The atmosphere we live in affects us. Painting and putting up attractive decorations can change the whole mood of a room. There is a good feeling to living in an environment that is pleasing to you and inviting to others. Our personal environment is often a reflection of our inner feelings. It's helpful to work on all levels.

POSITIVE ACTIONS: Helping and giving to others selflessly makes everyone feel better. When you see yourself doing good deeds, you feel better about yourself. The surest way to stop thinking about your own situation is to help someone who really needs help. If you use your creativity, innumerable ways of serving others can come to mind. For example, you can take flowers, cards, music, or even a smile and conversation to convalescent homes. You can volunteer time to a service organization. You can write positive messages on 3x5 index cards and post them around the office, at home or in supermarkets. You can say hello and send love to everyone you see or buy books that inspire you and give them to friends. The possibilities are limitless. It is more fun to do this sort of thing anonymously.

You can create a positive life through your thoughts, speech, company, environment and actions. To assist you, I highly recommend the following books:

I DESERVE LOVE by Sondra Ray
Les Femmes Publishing

HANDBOOK TO HIGHER CONSCIOUSNESS by Ken Keyes, Jr.
Living Love Center

THE LAZY MAN'S GUIDE TO ENLIGHTENMENT by Thaddeus Golas
The Seed Center

Nutrition and Attitudes

To stay charged with life-force, it is necessary to eat high quality natural foods and have positive attitudes. It is easier to maintain a good diet when it's backed by good attitudes. Likewise, it is easier to maintain positive attitudes while maintaining a good diet. But changing lifelong dietary habits can in some cases cause stress, and stress can nullify the benefits of an improved diet. The best approach to changing diet habits is to guide yourself gently and smoothly into new patterns of health and living. If changing your diet causes you physical or emotional stress, slow down and let the change happen at a pace you can handle. Enjoy yourself each step of the way.

The first three principles of good nutrition are related to one's attitudes.

1. *Eat when you are in a relaxed frame of mind.* In order to get the full value of the food you eat, do not eat when you are distressed or overly excited. If you must have something, drink juice or herbal tea.

2. *Feel good about what you eat and never criticize your food.* For most people, food satisfies some emotional needs. If you are going to eat something that you don't believe is good for you, at least enjoy it. If you enjoy it fully, it has the highest chance of being digested. Furthermore, you will neither crave the food as much, nor feel guilty about eating it.

3. *Allow yourself to eat whatever you want, whenever you want it.* As you begin a new dietary program, it is important not to deprive yourself of special treats you may desire. If you feel that you are denying yourself something, you will desire it more. We attract to ourselves the very things that we resist most. As an example, suppose a man wants to eat ice cream, but doesn't feel he should. Then, each time he says no to his desire for ice cream, the desire increases. On emotional levels he feels as if he is depriving himself of what he wants. Finally when the desire

wins out, he may end up eating ice cream excessively, and with feelings of guilt. The guilt is probably worse than the ice cream in the first place. If you know that you can have whatever you want whenever you want it, there will be no guilt over doing something wrong. Feel all right about yourself whatever you do, and moderation will come more easily.

4. *Substitute natural foods into your diet gradually.* If you are thinking of adding natural foods that you would enjoy to your diet, there need never be the feeling that you are missing or depriving yourself of anything. Every time you add something to your diet that you like, you get a good feeling without missing something you previously ate. New, healthy additions automatically mean that you have not eaten something else of probable lower quality. This helps assure that your new changes can take hold.

Another way of using substitution is in situations of craving. If you strongly desire some food you no longer think you should be eating, here is an option. First know that you can have it if you want it. Next, check with yourself and see if there is something else of higher quality that you would prefer more. For example, if someone craves ice cream, but stops and thinks for a moment, he or she might replace the ice cream craving with an even stronger desire for strawberries and yogurt. By substituting the higher quality food, we satisfy emotional and physical needs on a higher level of fulfillment.

5. *Food must be digested to be assimilated.* Food must first be digested before it can be of value to the cells. Undigested starches may ferment, and undigested proteins may putrify. This can become burdensome to the liver and can pollute the body. Here are some guidelines to easy digestion:

- *Eat when you are hungry.* When your body tells you to eat, your system is prepared for the intake of food. Your digestive fluids will be ready to go. Wait until you are hungry to eat a meal. Food eaten when you are hungry is more satisfying and more digestible, and therefore more nourishing and more gratifying. Eating a massive breakfast before you are hungry is not beneficial.
- *Eat moderately.* Moderation is essential for efficient digestion, assimilation, and good health. If your system is overloaded, it cannot

perform at peak levels. Try eating a bit less at each meal for starters. When you are excited about living, eating may be fun, but it is not the center of activity. Highly nutritional foods are more satisfying, so your cells may not put out that 'always hungry' message to your body.

6. *Eat high quality natural foods.* The highest quality foods are those that come to us in their most natural form. As we have noted, there is a universe of complexity within a cell. When man dares to tamper with his food, he runs the risk of changing things that he does not understand. Throughout the ages, animals and their food have evolved together in a delicate balance. No other animal but man has ever radically changed the nature of his food with fire, processing, preservatives, and the like. Animals in nature eat what is available from their environment in its raw natural form. For most, the diet is very simple.

Nutritional science is yet in its infancy. We know that there are carbohydrates, proteins, fats, vitamins, minerals, enzymes, and fiber, yet a major aspect of food seems to have been overlooked. That is the essential life-force in food. Almost every animal eats its food in a living' state. Herbivores eat grasses, seeds, and shrubs. Carnivores kill their meat and eat it fresh and raw. In doing this, animals assure themselves of obtaining the maximum life-force from their food. Life-force is a vital factor in high quality nutrition.

There is a major difference between natural foods and artificial ones. Currently, scientists say that there is no chemical difference between synthesized ascorbic acid and that naturally found in fruit. Perhaps they are missing the point. Holistic nutritionalists would say there is something more to discover. For example, current methods of detection have not found any chemical differences between a living person and a person immediately after death. The difference is in the life-force, not in the chemistry. Eating fresh food, rich in life-force, is different from eating canned food, although they may be chemically identical.

Cooking, processing, and preserving food changes the complex structure of the food we eat in many ways:
- life-force is destroyed.
- delicate enzymes are destroyed.

- fiber (necessary for healthy elimination) is broken down.
- simple sugars in foods are often converted into more complicated starches.
- many vitamins are destroyed.
- minerals can be lost.
- natural oils become saturated fats.

A simple first step to improve your diet is to gradually increase the amount of fresh raw fruits and vegetables you eat. Have at least one large mixed vegetable salad with sprouts each day. While you are doing this, cut back on your intake of sugar, honey, and alcohol as well as preserved, processed, and refined foods.

For more information, I highly recommend reading the works of Paavo Airola and Bernard Jensen. Both men have made wonderful contributions in the field of nutrition. See:

DOCTOR-PATIENT HANDBOOK by Bernard Jensen D.C., N.D.
Route 1, Box 52, Escondido, California 92025

ARE YOU CONFUSED by Paavo Airola N.D., Ph.D.

HOW TO GET WELL by Paavo Airola
Health Plus Publishers, Box 22001, Phoenix, Arizona 85028

Sharing The Gift

Now that you have had an opportunity
to work with the life-force
   —to experience it
   —to help, and to love
Now that you know . . .
      . . . you can begin to share.
You now have the tools to do what has never been done before—
To cross that bridge from spirit to science.

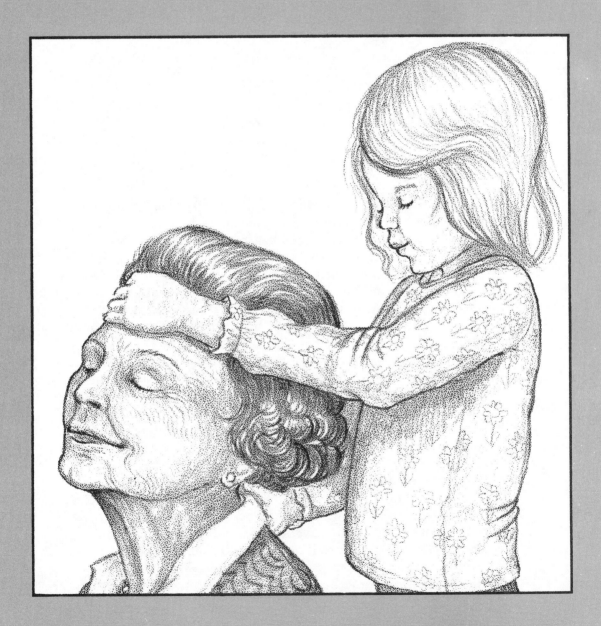

SECTION VI

Science and Life-Force

The use of life-force is ancient knowledge, but until recent times modern science has ignored or dismissed this phenomenon because of its association with religion or esoteric spiritualism. Newtonian physics was concerned with the mechanical behavior of material substance, and even the great Newton himself was uneasy about the spiritual implications of the invisible force of gravity. Nevertheless, the mechanical outlook was adopted by the medical profession. Anatomy classes in most medical schools still regard the human body as a highly sophisticated machine.

When Albert Einstein developed his famous formula $E = mc^2$ and showed that matter could be converted into energy, the dominant materialist outlook began to change in the scientific community. But medical science lagged behind, holding onto the mechanical concept of the human body and ignoring the body's energy interaction. The idea of life-force was taken seriously only by medical practitioners of the non-establishment holistic health movement, a group tolerated but hardly taken seriously by most physicians.

In recent years, radical changes in attitude have begun to take place because of extraordinary powers shown by a number of individuals. The telekinetic feats of Uri Geller, who is able to mentally move or bend objects such as metal keys or spoons, have been investigated by researchers at Stanford Research Institute, King's College in London, Kent State University, and the U.S. Defense Department. Olga Worrall, the internationally known spiritual healer, has proved in a number of university science laboratories that she can create turbulent waves inside cloud chambers—without touching them.* Beyond a doubt, it has been proved that some people have the ability to make use of life-force in ways that affect physical matter. It is also interesting that since Uri Geller began making public appearances, many other people have discovered they too have the same ability.

The tradition of healing by 'laying on of hands' goes back at least as far as Biblical times. This is not surprising, as life-force has been around as long as life itself! It is only because Western scientists have been so pre-occupied with looking into the properties of matter that they have overlooked the more subtle qualities of life-force.

"There are no 'things'; there are only interconnections," says Fritjof Capra, Ph.D., a physicist who has worked at the University of California and Stanford University research laboratories. In his book, *The Tao of Physics*, Dr. Capra discusses how energy relationships are the basis of both 'physical' and 'mental' phenomena. Now that scientists have recognized and have begun experimenting with life-force, it will not be long before the medical profession begins looking into this exciting opportunity.

Experts point out that the health care profession in this country is at a critical crossroad. Rising health care costs and increasing malpractice suits are pinching both doctors and patients, and neither group seems to know quite what to do about it. Historically, crises have served to point the way to new breakthroughs. Since most doctors are pragmatists, practical people willing to look at practical solutions to problems, they can be expected eventually to take effective processes like polarity energy balancing seriously. Life-force has been shown to be 'real', and polarity has pioneered in demonstrating many practical applications to health problems.

Life-force is an invaluable and inexhaustible natural resource—and it is free. Medical professionals who use it together with conventional therapy are likely to experience a greater degree of satisfaction among

*FOOTNOTE: A cloud chamber is an enclosed chamber used by scientists, which is supersaturated with vapor for revealing the presence of moving charged particles by their ionization of the vapor.

their patients and an accompanying drop in malpractice suit threats. Patients should rightly expect health care costs to be drastically reduced in cases of serious illness or injury. Everyone would benefit.

"The principles of polarity could be used as an intelligent foundation factor of agreement and procedure in all fields of therapy," wrote Dr. Randolph Stone, the founder of the modern polarity system. Because polarity relieves both physical and emotional suffering, its potential seems almost unlimited.

Applications

With a little thought, it is easy to suggest possible applications of polarity that would benefit both health and society. Here are some examples of applications that come to mind:

- for families to use as preventative care, or prior to medical attention during crises or emergencies
- in doctor's offices before and after medical treatment
- in hospitals to relieve suffering and ease tension
- in jails and mental institutions where inmates could practice on one another to restore and maintain a sense of well-being
- in schools, as basic education in conjunction with methods of first aid. Furthermore, when a child is misbehaving, the teacher could suggest a polarity. Instead of punishment, the child would receive the love of classmates.

Demonstration

To demonstrate polarity and the effects of life-force to the doubtful, the curious, or those simply interested in experiencing it, those techniques involving non-pressure or non-physical touch are the best. I suggest the following:

- The Cradle (see p. 38)
- The Tummy Rock (see p. 42)
- The Headache Move (see p. 22)
- The Finishing Moves (see p. 68)
- The Polarity Circle (see p. 112)

To maximize the results of your demonstration, here are three valuable tips:

1. Work on people who are hurting. Those who are strong and healthy may easily experience the life-force, but people who are hurting are likely to get dramatic relief from physical or emotional distress.

2. For optimum results, give polarity sessions when you are feeling strong and healthy.

3. Don't give a polarity after you or the other person you'll be working on has eaten a heavy meal. Some life-force is used in digesting food, so the effectiveness of the session could be reduced.

Polarity and the study of life-force are relatively new fields for investigation. Many fresh discoveries await those who choose to do the research. As yet, there are numerous basic questions to be answered. Here are a few which I feel deserve examination:

- Will the polarity circle help people who are dying be at peace in their final hours?
- Can a series of polarities control cancer?
- Why are some people more receptive to polarity therapy than others?
- What physiological changes occur during polarity sessions?
- How effective would a total and continuing program of polarity be in sustaining excellent health—particularly among those with records of chronic pain or frequent illness?

Two hundred years ago, when Benjamin Franklin flew his kite and had his famous experience with lightning, the force of lightning had always been around—but no one previously had been able to tap into it. When he did, people said, "Well, Ben, of what possible use is this electricity anyway?"

Life-force seems to be a subtle form of electricity that has about the same level of understanding that gross electricity had two hundred years ago. The possible uses of life-force could easily reshape the consciousness of humanity in the next hundred years more deeply than the use of electricity ever will.

For more information on polarity, the following organizations and individuals are suggested:

PIERRE PANNETIER POLARITY THERAPY CENTER
401 N. Glassell, Orange, California 92666
 (Pannetier is the successor of Dr. Randolph Stone, founder of polarity therapy.)
The following books by Dr. Stone are available from Pierre Pannetier:
For the lay reader desiring health maintenance information:
HEALTH BUILDING; SUMMARY; PURIFYING DIET and EASY STRETCHING POSTURES (4 books)
The remaining publications are technical textbooks:
Book I, ENERGY is a suggested introductory work pertaining to polarity
 philosophy.
Book III, POLARITY THERAPY, is a suggested introductory work pertaining to the practice of polarity therapy.

INTERNATIONAL POLARITY FOUNDATION
511 Main Street, Fort Lee, New Jersey 07024

DR. ED JARVIS (leading polarity practitioner)
572 Gibson, Pacific Grove, California 93950

The author, Richard Gordon, can also be contacted through Unity Press for those desiring more information.

Our Hands Are A Gift

Through them, we can channel the
love in our hearts to relieve the
suffering of those around us.

Biographical Note

Richard Gordon is a creative explorer in the holistic health field, with a gift for communicating concepts and facilitating people to experience their own potential as healers. As a practitioner of polarity energy balancing, Richard has evolved traditional polarity methods, combining them with innovative techniques like the 'Polarity Circle', now widely accepted since its introduction by Mr. Gordon. Richard has traveled extensively addressing professionals in the fields of medicine, mental health, education and holistic awareness. Currently he is participating in a Ph.D. dissertation project to demonstrate therapeutic applications of life-force using clinical diagnostic techniques.

More Unity Press books to further your integration.

THE GREAT AMERICAN MEDICINE SHOW
By Irving Oyle

Regarded by many as "the G.P. of the New Age of Medicine," Dr. Oyle draws from ancient healing lore, the latest in medical thought, and theoretical models of the new physics to describe in his most recent book modern medicine's approaching entry into the 21st century. *"We are not simply bodies,"* says Oyle. *"We are also fields of energy within which consciousness or mind is continually generating changes that affect what we call our state of health."*
$4.95 QUALITY PAPERBACK

LIFE TIME: A New Image of Aging
By Karen Preuss and William Henkin

A photo-documentary with text and exercises that probe beneath the deep-seated myth that the elderly cannot change. Using bio-feedback, Gestalt, yoga, massage and other relaxation and awareness techniques this book explores the aging process and makes us aware that it is not just the elderly that should be concerned with taking responsibility for their own lives. *"Involvement with activities as this book suggests is a great preparation for a new lifestyle."*
Maggie Kuhn, Gray Panthers
$6.95 QUALITY PAPERBACK

PLANET STEWARD: Journal of a Wildlife Sanctuary
By Stephen Levine

An award-winning journal compiled during the author's entrustment of a nature preserve. In this nesting place for over 125 species of birds and dozens of species of desert reptiles and mammals, Levine perceived the concept of planet stewardship; the meeting of ecological necessity and spiritual growth. *"Everyone needs to share the planet steward approach, whether he is concerned with a flower, a field, or a nation, and this book has brought us closer to that realization."* Huey Johnson
$4.95 QUALITY PAPERBACK